A Beginners Guide for Homeschooling
How to Set up a Successful Homeschool

Julia Groves   Donna Goff

A Beginner's Guide for Homeschooling

All rights reserved

No part of this book may be reproduced, or stored in a retrieval system, or transmitted in any form or by any means, electronic, mechanical, photocopying, recording, or otherwise, without express written permission of the publisher.

All rights reserved.

ISBN: 978-1-7354632-0-9

Cover design by: Rory R. Groves

Printed in the United States of America

Copyright © 2020 Magnitude Studios LLC

DEDICATION

This book is dedicated to all the amazing parents out there who are embarking on the adventure of homeschooling their children. You've got this!

A Beginner's Guide for Homeschooling

CONTENTS

Title Page
Copyright
Dedication

	Introduction	I
1	How to Legally Set Up Your Homeschool	Pg 1
2	Establishing a Solid Homeschool Foundation	Pg 11
3	Choosing your Homeschool Curriculum	Pg 23
4	Setting up the "School" part of your Homeschool	Pg 49
5	How to Address Socialization Needs	Pg 61
6	Establishing a Home Culture for Learning	Pg 71
7	Mom Care While Homeschooling	Pg 111
8	Homeschool Resources	Pg 121
	In Closing	Pg 137
	About the Authors	Pg 138

How to Set up a Successful Homeschool

INTRODUCTION

Are you looking into homeschooling your children? If so, you are not alone. Right now, over 2 million children are being homeschooled across the United States. Every parent who has chosen to homeschool their children has their own various reasons for doing so. However, two reasons that unite us all are that we love our children and believe that homeschooling is the best choice for them.

Choosing to homeschool your children is a big decision. However, once that choice is made, the question then becomes, **"Where do I start?"**

This is where A Beginners Guide for Homeschooling is here to help you. This book is not a practical guide in how to homeschool your children (we will be going into this in our next books). Rather, this book is here to walk you through step by step how to successfully ***set up*** your homeschool-- from how to make sure you are legally compliant with your state, to how to choose the right homeschool curriculum to fit your family's needs. By the time you read and apply what is found in the following pages, you will be ready to start actually homeschooling your children.

Before we get into the nitty-gritty of walking you through setting up a successful homeschool for your children, we would like to take a moment to introduce ourselves and our homeschooling background.

Hi, I am Donna Goff and I began homeschooling in the 1980s. Before I had children, I had never planned to homeschool. So, when I came to homeschooling, I did so reluctantly. It was before the internet and so I only had bookstores and libraries as my sources to figure it out. There were no support groups within about eighty miles! Because homeschooling was not my plan, I had no real plan except to pick up where they left off. I learned the hard way that this is not how to go about beginning homeschooling. This lack of planning resulted in my older children being in and out of public school.

My story would be really short had I firmly settled earlier on whether to either homeschool or public school. If I had it to do over, I would homeschool all of my children from the beginning, through high school, and not just my younger four children. I share my story, because I feel it pertains a lot to this book, to know my journey. I write this in hopes that you will benefit from my experiences.

When I only had two sons and a daughter, I found myself drawn into the early learning philosophy. I took a live week long detailed course in early childhood development. It was focused on how to enhance my children's development and early learning. The things I learned during that time have benefited all of my children. However, a lot of the early learning I found to be too tedious or not natural, as they involved flash cards. I did take the principles of clear focused repetition into my life and in teaching my children. When my daughter was two, we tried doing a play based preschool. All the moms wanted to add academics. As we did not know any better, we added academics. We did preschool for one semester.

Later, I had four more children but armed with more information, I chose not to do preschool at home, nor did I send my children to preschool. I focused more on providing support for healthy development.

My older three children attended kindergarten. I had no idea the law did not require it in the state where I lived. In talking to the principal, he suggested I homeschool! I gave him my notice and two weeks later I started homeschooling my oldest, he was in fourth grade.

We moved and by Christmas I was homeschooling all of them, kinder, third, and fourth grade. That summer I had my fourth child and because of this sent my oldest children back to public school where they attended for the next two years. I had my fifth child and decided to try homeschooling my children again. However, before long, I was exhausted and sleep deprived from a newborn. My husband re-enrolled our older children in public school. I must say I felt guilty and felt like I had failed.

We moved to Utah. I enrolled my three oldest children in public school. However a few months later my daughter begged to just be homeschooled. I understood why she requested to be homeschooled so I agreed to her request. As we left the school that day, we walked by the kindergarten classroom. I pointed it out to her younger sister who replied, "That's fine for them mom, I have something better."

At that instant, I realized I was into homeschooling for the long haul. I invested time in learning about models, philosophies, methods, and connecting with other homeschoolers. I had my sixth child.

A Beginner's Guide for Homeschooling

My oldest two who didn't want to be homeschooled, chose to do independent study and graduated from high school early. I then had a seventh child. My oldest daughter was homeschooled from sixth grade through graduation. My youngest four children were homeschooled to adulthood.

In this book, I want to share from my experience and help you to begin your homeschool journey. Starting out right can mean a world of difference in how your homeschool flows.

Hi, my name is Julia Groves (I am Donna Goff's oldest daughter). As my mother previously stated, my first personal experience with homeschooling was when I was in kindergarten when my parents for a brief time pulled my older brothers out of the public school system (due to issues at their school) and opted to homeschool them. I enjoyed joining in on their studies. I have a particular memory from that time of my father teaching my older brothers and I how to add large numbers together. He taught us on this huge white board. I remember feeling so grown up that I knew how to add really big numbers together.

Anyway, while that was my first homeschool experience, my official homeschool journey didn't begin for several more years. It began in the middle of my 6th grade year. That is when I begged my mother one day to let me come home to be homeschooled full time. There were a number of reasons for this personal request. The main one being I had no desire to skip another grade (which was being discussed) as I was getting bullied enough for having already done so at my last school.

I decided that I wanted to come home and take charge of my own education. I wanted to really study the subjects I was interested in, rather than just skimming the surface as we were doing in school. I wanted peace away from all the bullies. My mother seeing the writing on the wall agreed to my request and that's how I ended up being homeschooled from the 6th-grade year through high school. (Though I did take a few classes at our local high school with my friends. I even performed in a school play at our local high school thanks to the kindness a understanding drama teacher)

Looking back I have never regretted my decision to be homeschooled even though it came with it's own set of trials. (The main one being that homeschooling wasn't aas widespread or accepted back then, so I got a lot of push back from my friends and their parents.) No, I never doubted or regretted my choice to be homeschooled. In fact, I am very grateful I had the opportunity.

Later on, after attending a couple semesters at private liberal arts college I taught for a short time at private elementary school before stepping away from formally teaching in order to raise my own family. However, through the years I have enjoyed speaking at various Homeschool conferences to both youth and adults.

Now I have 3 kids of my own who I am currently homeschooling together with my husband. I have to say that homeschooling isn't always the easiest educational choice, but it can be the most rewarding. I love teaching my kids and learning from them. But what I really love is that the world is our school. We can go anywhere and learn as we go. We have freedom.

We invite you to join in the journey! It will be work, but it will be so worth it to homeschool your children.

1. HOW TO LEGALLY SET UP YOUR HOMESCHOOL

Let's assume that you have officially decided to homeschool your children. Now what? It is natural when taking a big step like homeschooling, to ask for direction and advice from those who have already successfully done so. That's why you are reading this book isn't it? After all, why reinvent the wheel. If someone can help you have a better homeschool experience, then why not ask them? This is why, If you have friends or family who homeschool, we of course recommend that you talk to them. Go and get ideas and find support for your decision.

However, as you do so, please be aware that what works for one family may not always be the best course for your family. Additionally, it is important to understand that there are laws you need to be compliant with in order to homeschool.

When you wanted to send your children to a public or private school, you needed to enroll them. Now that you are looking at homeschooling your children, it is very important to be aware that there are official procedures that you are required to follow to establish your homeschool. Homeschool laws differ from state to state. Some states have very low regulations when it comes to homeschooling while others have very high strict regulations. Trust m, when I tell you it is very important to know the homeschool laws for where you live and to always be compliant.

Imagine this scenario. June lives in New York and decided that she is going to homeschool her children. The first thing she does after making her decision is to call up her sister Alice who has been homeschooling for years. Alice, who lives in Utah, is soo excited that her sister is going to homeschool her children. So, Alice is quick to assure her sister that transitioning to homeschooling is a piece of cake. All she has to do is send in an affidavit to her school district listing her kids' names, letting them know that she is going to homeschool. Then Alice advises her sister June not to worry about picking a homeschool curriculum right away. She tells her that she should let her kids unschool for a bit when they start to help her kids adjust to homeschooling life.

June figures that her sister knows what she is talking about. After all, Alice has homeschooled her children for several years now. So, June does what her sister tells her to do. Weeks later, while June is playing some fun educational games with her kids, there is a knock on the door. On the other side of the door is a social worker and a police officer who had come to find out why June's kids are delinquent from school. June tells them she is homeschooling her kids. To which she is quickly informed that her kids are not officially on record as homeschooling. June tells them she sent in a letter stating her intent to homeschool wasn't that enough?

Imagine June's surprise and horror to discover that in the state of New York it is not. In fact, she isn't complying with any of the homeschool laws in her state. This is a serious matter which is why the police and the social worker were called in. Eventually, everything is straightened out but now June has a very bad taste in her mouth about homeschooling.

Had June read this book, she would have realized that there are specific laws for homeschooling in every state. She would have looked up the laws for where she lived before she asked for specific homeschool advice from her sister. She would have followed the requisite laws from the beginning, and would then most likely have had no problems with the police or social workers for her homeschooling.

This book is here as a resource for you so you do not make June's mistake. The following information in this chapter will show you how to find out the laws in your area and how to file your official homeschool affidavit.

HOW TO FIND OUT THE HOMESCHOOL REQUIREMENTS IN YOUR STATE

Yes, there is a legal side to homeschooling and it is important that you do this part properly. The difficulty is that every state in the United States has different laws and regulations for homeschooling. So, what are the homeschool laws in your state? And if you were to experience legal issues with homeschooling, who would you call?

We would highly recommend checking out the Home School Legal Defense Association at hslda.org. This site is a national homeschool resource. There you will find a legal summary of the homeschool laws and regulations for every state in the Union. They really do a good job at keeping up with the constantly changing landscape of homeschool laws in each state. Additionally, for those who pay to be a part of their association, they offer legal help in the case that you have any homeschool legal issues.

You can also go to your state homeschool organization websites to find current information on laws and regulation for homeschooling where you live. They usually can help you locate the actual wording of your state homeschool and private school laws. This is a good thing to look into.

For example, did you know that in some states, homeschoolers have more autonomy as a private school.

You would find this information on your state homeschool organization site.

Below are some of the laws and regulations you will want to know about before you start homeschooling:

COMPULSORY ATTENDANCE AGE

Are your children under the compulsory school age for your state? If so, you may not have to do anything... yet. Currently, the compulsory school attendance laws in the various states range in age between five to eight years. At this time, no state requires preschool and 80% of states do not require kindergarten at age five.

So, if your child is between the ages of five and eight, check your state compulsory attendance age first thing.

After you determine if your children are of compulsory age and have checked with your state laws for how to file with your state and local school district to officially homeschool, there are other things to consider.

TIME

Does your state require a certain number of days or hours of school a year? Many states have laws stating that 180 days are required of school each year. Some states require school to be in session during the school day. If your state does require homeschool during the same hours as public school, what is their provision for field trips and recess?

RECESS

Recess is vital, especially in the elementary years. Find out if you need to be outside in the back yard with your children during recess time. For some states are free range states and children of certain ages do not need a parent present during recess while others this is not the case.

CURRICULUM

Does your State require you to provide for approval a written homeschool curriculum? Or does your state require you to create a homeschool plan? Even if they do not, it is a good idea to create one.

Some states require you to work with a coordinator, to verify your plan or curriculum meets their guidelines. Some states require approval of your plan. Does your state have required subjects? If they require subjects, they usually leave it up to you on how you will teach that subject, how often, what content you use, and what resources or curriculum you use to teach those areas.

SOCIAL INTERVENTION

Some states, out of an abundance of caution, have social workers assigned to visit new parents. There are some states that do the same for homeschoolers. This is automatic, it's not based on being reported to social services. This is just something you have to be prepared to deal with in those states.

Then in other states such as mine, social workers are not

involved with homeschooling. In fact, our state law removed homeschooling from the list of reporting to social services. In our state, if we homeschool, the district is prohibited from inspecting our home and our curriculum. Does your state require intervention with a social worker?

TESTING

Does your state require testing? A few states test all students every year. Others test every other year. And still others have no testing requirement for homeschooling at all. unless you choose to re-enroll your children in public or private school. In this circumstance the testing is done to know where to properly place your children being readmitted into public/private/charter school.

When you are working one-on-one with a student, it is easier to see what they grasp easily and where they struggle. Standardized tests do not reveal hesitancy. They only test in relation to other children the same age. Yet, children do not learn and develop by age.

If your state does not require standardized testing, we would recommend you forgo them. They are actually designed to test and compare children in a classroom. Some countries that are performing better than the US on international tests, have zero standardized testing until graduation. There are many ways to test progress. We will discuss them later in the book.

If your state requires testing, it is good to be aware of what the tests are, how often they need to be administered, and who administers them.

RECORDS

What records does your state require homeschoolers keep? Many states require attendance records and some require vaccine records. A few states require you to work with a coordinator and also require you compile a portfolio of samples of your children's work. Keeping a good record of progress is important for you, even when a state does not require one. *Later in this book we will cover a simple and in depth way to keep your homeschool records.*

HOMESCHOOL AFFIDAVITS

Affidavits are basically the name for the legal document that you need to submit to your local school district to remove your kids from public school to officially homeschool them. Some states have state-mandated forms to sign when beginning homeschool. While other states will allow you to make your own notarized affidavits and a few don't require any written notice of intent to homeschool at all. Some states require you to file every year. Some states require you to only have to refile when you change your address.

We live in a state that requires a notarized affidavit submitted to your local school district in order to homeschool. However, In our state the law just says we need to file once. The law does not say the school district is to create a form. Our state only requires us to file an affidavit once, unless we move.

In the case that you are allowed to write your own homeschool affidavit for your children. We recommend writing what we call a "lean affidavit". What is a lean affidavit?

A LEAN AFFIDAVIT

A "lean" affidavit is one that contains the minimum information required by law. These laws are there to protect your privacy and the privacy of your children. Sometimes, school districts create a form, for "convenience." Sadly, sometimes they ask for more information than the law entitles them to receive from you. Remember, less is more. It is best not to volunteer more information than the law requires. When we do give more than is required because the questions seem to be innocuous, we set precedence and schools can begin to demand more. So, go to your state law and discover what your state requires.

Take time to learn about your state's homeschool law and start homeschooling in a safe way. Discover the compulsory school ages, time, recess, curriculum, social intervention, testing, and record keeping requirements of your state's law and how to officially apply to homeschool.

2. ESTABLISHING A SOLID HOMESCHOOL FOUNDATION

You now understand how to legally homeschool in your state. Before you run out and buy a curriculum, don't make the same mistake that many do (and that I even did). Don't homeschool without a plan. A plan will help provide a context for your homeschooling. A plan makes it easier to assess progress.

Imagine that your homeschool is a building. Every builder knows that before they can break ground to pour the foundation or actually start building the actual structure it is important to have clear blueprints to know what they are building. This is why construction companies hire skilled architects to make detailed blueprints. These blueprints guide the workers to know what to put where, as they work, and what the building is supposed to look like when finished. If you want to be successful in the homeschool you are building, having a clearly defined blueprint will help you stay on course.

Let me explain this concept in another way. In the Business World, this blueprint is called a business plan. This business plan will often include details of why the business is being created (what needs the business is filling). It includes their vision of how they want to accomplish their goals. And it also includes details of foreseen obstacles and how they plan to address them.

Your homeschool is your business. Having a well thought out and written down homeschool business plan will help give you the edge in the homeschool world. It will keep you on track with your homeschool goals and give you the clarity you need when you face those inevitable obstacles to overcome them. And, it will help you to know when you have succeeded in your homeschool endeavor.

DEFINING YOUR HOMESCHOOL WHY

We all have a reason why we chose to homeschool. For some, it is because they have children who have special needs that they feel can be better met at home. For others, it is because they don't approve of the public school curriculum, agenda or atmosphere. For others still, it is for health reasons. And again for others, choose to homeschool because they believe their children will learn better at home with the world as their classroom. Often, you will find that you have more than one reason why. Ultimately, we all share one main Why. Namely that we love our children and feel that homeschooling is the best option for them.

It is important to take the time to define and articulate your why. We can guarantee you that you will need to remind yourself of your, time and again throughout your homeschool journey. Yes, you will need to remind yourself of your why when you hit opposition to your choice, as well as when homeschooling becomes difficult. Even the best of kids have bad days or weeks and reminding yourself why you are homeschooling will give you the strength to push through and keep going.

When sitting down to define your why ask yourself why are you homeschooling? What brought you to this point? Why is homeschooling your best option right now? Get a notebook, journal, or binder. Write down your why for homeschooling. Again, there will be times that you will struggle and wonder why you are doing this. Going back to your written "whys" will help you regain the clarity as well as the courage needed to face those difficulties.

At one point, I prayerfully brainstormed all the good, bad and ugly I could think of that had to do with public, private, and homeschool. I then crossed off anything that was on every option. Then I counted up and homeschool won. I was shocked, but felt at peace with my choice.

Later on while homeschooling there were great days and not so great days. My husband on more than one occasion said, "Why don't we just put them back in public school for someone else to deal with." On those occasions, I countered by reminding us both of our why and the choice to remain homeschooling won every time.

Your why has power!

ASSESSING WHERE YOU ARE & ANY SPECIAL NEEDS

Before you can create your homeschool plan you need to assess where you, your children and your family are, and any special needs you may have.

When we mention assessing, most people think we are just talking about figuring out at what level your children are in regards to various educational subjects they are required to master before they can graduate. Or they think about where their children's skills are at. While that is important, that is not what we are talking about here.

We have created a basic assessment for you to really show where you are and how you are doing.

We would recommend that both you and your spouse discuss the questions below and then write down your answers together in a notebook or binder.

FIRST START WITH YOU AND YOUR SPOUSE:

1. What are your personal strengths?

2. What areas of your life do you feel needs strengthening?

NOW LOOK AT EACH INDIVIDUAL CHILD IN YOUR HOME:

1. What are their strengths? *We want to focus on areas they are doing well, as this is where they gain confidence.*

2. Does your child have any ***special*** needs?

3. What are you doing to address those special needs?

4. What are your child's individual needs?

5. What is your child's personality?

6. What is your child's attention span?

7. Has your child been trained in good work habits and habitudes (habitual atitudes?

8. How do you plan to address needs, personalities, attention span, work habits, and habitudes of your children?

9. What areas do they need strengthening? *Realize that some of this may deal with their development and will take time to strengthen.*

NOW IT'S TIME TO ASSESS YOUR FAMILY?

1. What do you feel are your family's strengths? What are you rocking as a family? Keep enjoying these things.

What areas of family life do you feel needs strengthening?

Brainstorm ways to strengthen those areas of your family life, in need of strengthening, or bringing focus to.

DEFINING YOUR HOMESCHOOL VISION.

There is one last step you need to take before you start to create your homeschool business plan. Now that you have your why defined and your needs assessed, it is time to clarify your vision. You can map your journey if you do not have your sight on a destination. So, that is why the next step is to define your vision or your target for your homeschool.

It is said in Proverbs that "where there is no vision, the people perish." So what are you envisioning for your homeschool?

THE QUESTIONS BELOW ARE TO HELP YOU DEFINE AND REFINE YOUR VISION:

1. What is your homeschool vision for you?

2. How do you envision yourself in a decade?

3. What is your vision for your family?

4. What is your idea of a perfect homeschool day?

5. When you think about the future, how do you envision your children as adults?
    - What will they be like because they were raised in your home and homeschooled?
    - Will they lead out and even stand alone on principle?
    - What is your vision of them? Write it down.

Childhood lasts until your children are eighteen years old. It is not a race to adulthood. You have time and so do they. Isn't it refreshing to know that they won't be adults tomorrow. Let's be real, our children have heaps of growing to do between now and then. When you have a clear vision you know where to aim. It is easier to stay the course and work through difficulties, as they arise.

Writing down your vision has power to make it happen. Keep your vision with your why and your official plan in an accessible binder for you will refer to it often.

CREATING YOUR HOMESCHOOL BUSINESS PLAN

Yey! Now it is finally time to start your official homeschool business plan! Another way to view your homeschool plan is as a road map. A road map shows you all the different possible routes to get from where you are to your desired destination. Road maps are full of possibilities! When you get to a roadblock your map can help you to see alternate routes to your destination.

Back to our business plan analogy. In a business, the business plan helps give focus and clarity to the growth and development of the business, likewise a Homeschool Business Plan helps you develop and grow your homeschool.

Just remember that both your family and your education are a work in progress. Which is why your homeschool plan will really be a work in progress as well. You will add to it as you learn more and you may remove things that no longer are meaningful to you as you go along.

While some parents may be tempted to skip this step. Others will take it seriously and it will benefit their families no matter where their children learn, at home or public, private or charter school.

Your business plan will start with your defined Why, Vision while taking into account what you recorded in your assessment. Now it is time to think about the practical application for your homeschool.

Like home culture, family libraries, preparedness, and events that you want your family to experience, have and attend.

We will be going through these subjects later in this book so keep note for you will most likely want to add them to your homeschool business plan.

Now that you have a good idea of how to homeschool legally, you have assessed, created a vision and a Homeschool Business Plan. In this context you can explore now homeschool philosophy, methods, models and curriculum you will use to teach your children.

3 CHOOSING YOUR HOMESCHOOL CURRICULUM

Choosing what curriculum to use with your children can be a big decision. When you use a curriculum that is the right fit for your family, then your job as a homeschool parent is made so much easier. On the other hand, trying to use a curriculum that is not the right fit for your family can easily lead to burn out for both you and your children.

Added to this is the fact that many good homeschool curriculums are not cheap. Which is understandable considering all the work that goes into creating them.

When you combine all these concerns together it is easy to understand why so many homeschool parents worry about finding the right curriculum to invest in.

Don't worry, this book is here to help you do just that. We won't tell you what exact curriculum to use in your homeschool, for what you choose will depend greatly on factors that we will be addressing shortly.

The first thing you need to understand, when it comes to homeschool curriculums is that there is no such thing as a perfect curriculum. There is no silver bullet as they say. Many parents have gotten sucked into the rabbit hole of searching for that perfect curriculum and have subsequently spent thousands of dollars doing so and have never gotten around to actually using what they have.

Let us explain with a story: Years ago a friend called in panic. My friend was sucked in to researching daily for the best resources for homeschooling. She had selected and purchased what she felt were the most popular curriculums for each subject. My friend did not know how to orchestrate it all to teach her children. I invited her to lunch after a community President's Day event. As I drove home from the event, this parable came to me. What she was struggling with is a common dilemma for many homeschool parents, homeschooling without a plan.

THE PARABLE OF THE EMPTY HARVEST

There once was a farmer that lived on the outer edge of a small city. Each summer, he would plant his fields in corn. The people in the city loved his corn. His acreage was quite large. It was too difficult to grow many different types of crops. So he chose to specialize in growing corn. He had to use large farm machinery and a commercial irrigation system to get all of the work done. The farmer built a large barn to store his machinery in. His farm was efficient. He always had a good crop for the summer farmer's market in the city.

To the west of this farm was a small neighborhood. A certain man, from that neighborhood, was out for a walk one day. He viewed the beautiful corn plants, in nicely spaced rows. This man decided right then and there, that he would start a garden. Inspired by the lovely corn fields, this man went off to the city to purchase all of the needed supplies. The gardener went to a hardware store and purchased small scale farm equipment to set up a small corn farm in his backyard. He went to a plant nursery and bought a bag of the same kind of corn seed and chemicals that the farmer used. He went home and got to work.

First, he tore out the velvety green lawn in his backyard and tilled the earth. He installed an automatic water irrigation system. He planted his corn and felt very happy. He could almost taste the corn! He was now a "new gardener."

The 'new gardener" took another walk on a fine sunny day. He walked past his neighbor to the south. The neighbor's gate was open and his neighbor waved to him and bid him come. When he got to his neighbor's backyard, he saw the most colorful garden he had ever seen. It was not planted in rows. It was planted in neat little square foot grow boxes. He had sixty-four corn plants growing in a 4 x 4 foot square. They were a short season corn that produced two corn ears per stalk. He had a salad garden, lined in flowers. He had a canning garden, with trellised tomatoes and beans. His garden was beginning to come into its first harvest of the season. This was the garden that fed his neighbor and his neighbor's wife. They had no expensive equipment. They hand watered from 5 gallon buckets that they let sit out all day, so they would not shock the plants. There were not that many weeds, because the square foot gardener had made his own soil. They composted and rebuilt the soil.

Now this made our "new gardener" excited. He went home and yanked up all of his corn plants, then put his tools and sprinkler system in the shed. He then went out to purchase all he needed to set up a square foot system in his backyard. He came home, built the grow boxes, and then planted his seeds. He was proud of all the pretty boxes.

In July the "new gardener" took another walk. He saw that the farmer had lovely knee high corn. The "new gardener" went walking through his neighborhood. The "new gardener" was weary. His plants did not look as good as his neighbor to the south. When he had looked at his neighbor's square-foot garden, it had looked so beautiful and easy. His neighbor and his wife to the south had no children and managed their garden without much effort. The "new gardener" on the other hand, has seven children. He had planted more grow boxes than his neighbor. The hand watering was hard to keep up, and the clipping of weeds from stray seeds had fallen behind.

Then our "new gardener" walked by his neighbor to the north. The neighbor to the North had a medium size family. So the "new gardener" peaked over the fence. There was a green house in his back yard. This neighbor to the north used a hydroponics system. No weeds! Food year around! The "new gardener" knew that this was the answer. He ran home full of hope. Yes, you guessed it. He pulled out his entire square foot system; plants and all! He put all of the parts in the shed. He went into town and purchased a large greenhouse. He went to the hardware store and bought more tools. He went to the garden shop and bought liquid plant food and seeds. He went home and set the whole operation into action. Boy was it impressive! He was joyful.

In August, the "new gardener" took another walk. Oh my! The farmer to the east had harvested his corn and took it to market. The square foot gardener was getting his third crop in. His greenhouse neighbor had a lush garden. The "new gardener" was tired. The green house had proven to be too much work; measuring nutrients, watching the temperature, opening and closing vents. What was our "new gardener" to do?

He then noticed his neighbor to the east. That neighbor had a huge family and a wonderful garden. The neighbor to the east had long raised beds, covered with fabric mulch to keep the weeds away, and a drip irrigation system. He fed his plants colloidal minerals in a water solution. These indeed were healthy plants. The "new gardener" thought," no weeds, large plants, no watering hassles (it is on a timer), almost no work!" "This has got to be the best system ever devised!" he thought. So, home he went. Down came the green house. The shed was full, so he stacked everything outside. Out came all of the plants too. Back into town he went. Home he came with everything he needed. He worked long and hard. Finally, everything was planted. He could rest now. The plants would practically grow themselves.

Harvest time came, but not for our "new gardener." While his neighbors all picked a method and worked it with consistency, our "new gardener" had been unwise. Ever looking for something better, he was always changing to a better method. The winter came and he had nothing to harvest. His shed was full of partially used equipment. His plants were too young to harvest. He had spent all his time, money and energy trying to have the best garden. To make matters worse he had tried to rush things. He poured a whole season's worth of fertilizer on the garden one day. He did not have time to get the water going, he would work out that automatic system on Saturday. He could flood it then, to make up with the lack of watering. After all, it worked for the Chinese and their rice paddies. Well, he burned the crop and then drowned it. He was left with an empty harvest; and he was sad.

Are we like this unwise gardener?

When I told my friend the parable, she stopped me at greenhouses. She was excited. She had bought a greenhouse in a box and it needed to be put together. She instantly thought she could let her son put it together for homeschool. While that was a brilliant idea, she was missing my point. So, I finished the parable and then I interpreted the parable. So, I provide the parable interpretation here.

THE PARABLE OF THE EMPTY HARVEST II

Everyone can see how foolish the "new gardener" was. Each system he tried would have worked had he stayed with it. All would have yielded a harvest. Perhaps some harvests would have been better than others; but they all would have had a harvest.

The farmer represents mass schooling systems, both public and private. To teach enormous groups of children they use a one size fits all education. Many home school families, following this model, have actually had better success then the schools themselves do.

The square foot gardener represents Leadership Education. The harvest from this method is very fine. This approach can be used even with larger families. It takes time and dedication to implement.

The greenhouse were private schools. This too yields a fine harvest.

The raised bed gardener represented a living education like Charlotte Mason. This too yields a harvest.

Many of us jump from curriculum to curriculum. We have accumulated rooms of "buyer's remorse". We could free ourselves from guilt and sell it all on the internet. Less is more. Consistently applied effort in any of these methods will bring a glad harvest. We need to take stock. We need to weigh out the options, wisely choose the model, philosophy, materials and methods to use.

The Charlotte Mason philosophy helps you eat the elephant one bite at a time. It covers the typical school subjects and more; and in the way children naturally learn. It can be taught one on one or in a group. I find it freeing. But you need to choose what system works best with you and your family, and then consistently do it. We also have got to stop this perfectionistic craziness of always looking for the best or perfect curriculum. It does not exist. Educational theories are in constant change. We need to see that we will never harvest, if we cannot consistently apply anything. It is time for a story. Wild Day Time! It is time for a nature walk! Do school each day. The sanity you save may be your own. Do not try to catch up. Learning is a continuum. Trying to cram learning will only drown and burnout your tender children. Just place one foot in front of the other and be consistent in moving forward. Remember that the tortoise learned that slow and steady wins the race! If you keep moving it is amazing what little bites here and little bites there will accomplish.

Yes, there is a lesson here that no matter what curriculum you choose, stick with it at least for a season to see what harvest you get before trying something new if you are dissatisfied with your results. However, I would advise before jumping to a new curriculum next year, to first evaluate how you are applying the curriculum you have. As well as your home culture routines because that can vastly affect your results.

Now before we talk about actual homeschool curriculums on the market, to help you know which one will be a good fit for you and your family, it's important to understand homeschool models, philosophies, and methods. When you have a clear idea of what models, philosophies, and methods resonate with you it will be easier to pick a curriculum for your family or even make your own combining parts of multiple curriculums and resources available.

DECIDING ON YOUR HOMESCHOOL MODEL

When it comes down to it, there are basically three major models of education. You have the Age Grade Learning model, the Non- Age Grade Mastery learning model and the Self-Directed Un-schooling model. For those not familiar with these three education models we will discuss them below so that you can see which model resonates the most with you.

AGE GRADE BASED MODEL

The age or grade based model is the model most public schools and private schools of the 20th Century used. This model was designed to graduate everyone from high school at eighteen. In this model children are divided by age and move from grade to grade with their age peers.

While this may seem like a very efficient model, studies and tests have shown that in most first grade classrooms there is usually a four to five-year spread of child development. In other words, in any given first grade class you will find children who are 1-2 years behind grade level and 1-2 years above grade level in understanding, development and skill. By the fifth grade this gap in understanding and skill increases to six to eight years for each class. That is a wide range of understanding, skills, and development in just one class for a teacher who is responsible for 25-40 students to address.

This is why In the age or grade model of education, their skill curriculum is usually a spiral curriculum. These spiral curriculums are designed to spend a lot of time reteaching and catching up students before moving on to new content. That is fine if your child is behind, but what if your child is ahead?

On another note about this educational model, a new large study from Stanford and Berkley universities show that by delaying school entry until seven for kindergarten can eliminate (*according to their claims*) over 73% of ADHD symptoms up until age 11.5. This leads you to question if a lot of ADHD symptoms we see today are actually a stress response to developmentally inappropriate education. Or to wonder if many children with ADHD symptoms are merely showing these symptoms because they are delayed in foundational development, due to the substituting of early education for what most children need for healthy development. ***Just some food for thought.***

THE NON-GRADED/MASTERY MODEL

Now let us move on to the non-graded model. This model has prevailed over the centuries. This model typically includes play-based kindergarten. Non-graded schools are mastery based. This model has been used by private tutors, elite academies, governesses, mentors, cottage schools, common schools, and even one-room school houses.

The non-graded One-Room School House Model is also known as Developmentally Appropriate Practice (DAP), Continuous Learning Model, or Continuous Growth Model. In this model, general knowledge is taught to everyone together, because general knowledge is not skill based and is non-sequential, by its very nature. Rudiments and skill development are ability grouped.

In the home, this means a child's developmental readiness dictates the pace of learning. Children are taught in a manner that builds one concept upon another. Children are also free to engage in self-selected, self-directed, independent, interest-led learning, which naturally develops the skills they were learning. Children in this model can often experience outdoor life and recess, which helps develop their attention span, brain, and body for learning.

According to Barbara Nelson Pavan, in The Benefits of Non-Graded Schools, students in non-graded schools perform better on both standardized tests and mental health assessments in 52 out of 57 studies. While this model is centuries old, it is also very twenty-first century. Clearly the mastery model is a viable option for homeschoolers.

SELF-DIRECTED/UNSCHOOLING MODEL

Lastly, let us discuss the Self-directed, Interest-led Unschooling model. This is a model where children learn naturally, in the context of the need to know, self-directed learning from everyday life. Children learn through relationships with people and things. Children engage in projects of interests, learn what they need to know, and develop skills. This is the oldest model of learning and the least structured though very efficient.

Which model fits your vision for your family?

DECIDING ON YOUR HOMESCHOOL PHILOSOPHY

It is important to note that while there are many philosophies to homeschooling, most are built on one of the above models. However, depending on how one implements a philosophy, it can be fit in more than one model.

Let's discuss the top educational philosophies that fit within each of the three main educational models addressed above.

PHILOSOPHIES THAT FIT WITHIN THE AGE-GRADE BASED MODEL INCLUDE:

ONLINE DISTANCE LEARNING AND K-12 APPROACH

Both Online Distance Learning and K-12 programs are public school education delivered over the internet into the home. These programs fit squarely within the Age-Grade Model.

SCHOOL AT HOME APPROACH

The School at Home Approach also uses the public school model, methods, timing, workbooks and texts to recreate a school in the home.

THE LOUIS BENEZET PHILOSOPHY

The Louis Benezet Philosophy can be used in the graded or non-graded classroom. He believed that children were going through math and language arts before they had a solid foundation. In elementary school, he restricted math to the math children needed to know on a practical level for their age, and reserved abstract math for seventh grade. He promoted oral composition as pre-composition, in the elementary years. Benezet delayed the teaching of language arts until seventh grade. Then in junior high, students were taught the rudiments of math, spelling, and grammatical conventions of our language.

CHARLOTTE MASON PHILOSOPHY

The Charlotte Mason Philosophy was designed to be used in graded classrooms. Yet she also ran an international support called the Parents National Education Union. There she helped parents adopt her philosophy and methods to homeschooling and in a family style learning. So, the Charlotte Mason Philosophy can be used through both the Age- Grade Model or the Non Age Grade Model. Many call this a Living Education. This philosophy uses quality literature, and is also rich in history, arts, and nature studies. This is hands-on, contextual learning. Charlotte Mason delayed academics until first grade.

ROBINSON PHILOSOPHY

Robinson Philosophy is designed for children to teach themselves independently within the structure of grade levels.

AMERICAN CLASSIC PHILOSOPHY

The American Classic Philosophy is grade-based, using texts once used in 19th Century American community schools and one-room school houses, such as McGuffey's Readers, Winston Grammar, Ray's Arithmetic, Carpenter's Geography, and Spencerian Script. These American classics can be used in a Mastery Model.

WELL TRAINED MIND APPROACH

Well Trained Mind is classical education divided by grades. (See Classical Education under the non-graded model. Grammar stage is taught in elementary school. Logic stage is taught in middle school. Rhetoric stage is taught in high school.

PRINCIPLE APPROACH

Principle Approach or Noah Plan, after Noah Webster, is based on teaching the seven principles of liberty through great literature and history. While this is often arranged by grade, the Noah Plan or Principle Approach when done as homeschool, can be a non-graded one room school.

Note: that some of these philosophies, depending on implementation can also fit in another philosophy model. Often these philosophies have their own unique teaching methods. These methods can also be used in a non-graded model.

PHILOSOPHIES THAT FIT IN THE NON-GRADED MODEL INCLUDE:

COTTAGE SCHOOL APPROACH

Cottage School is a one room school in someone's home. There are no grade divisions. General Knowledge is taught together, skills are learned one on one, or depending on the number of students, ability grouped between beginner and advanced students.

CLASSICAL EDUCATION PHILOSOPHY

Classical Education is the Latin Trivium. This model was designed as a non-graded model of three stages of learning, before advanced learning. The Grammar stage is where the mechanics of language and subjects are taught. The Logic stage is where the mechanics of thought and analysis are taught. The Rhetoric Stage is the application stage, where grammar and logic meet, and are used to persuade. This philosophy can be used in other models.

CHARLOTTE MASON PHILOSOPHY

The Charlotte Mason Philosophy when done in a homeschool, can be implemented as a non-graded one room school, cottage school, or family style learning. In other words, Charlotte Mason Philosophy can be used in a Non-graded, Mastery Model.

LEADERSHIP EDUCATION PHILOSOPHY

Leadership Education is a principle based philosophy where children progress through phases of learning. Core phase is the foundational phase where core identity and core values are developed through working, playing, worshipping together as a family. Goals of the Love of Learning phase to fall in love with learning. Transition to scholar, usually happens in the middle years. Here they develop scholar skills, as well as a breadth of knowledge. Scholar phase is where they build on the foundation of their core phase and where their love of learning carries them through broadening their learning and deepening their learning. Towards the end of their scholar years they evaluate areas of learning they need to develop. They formulate their own plan and fill their academic holes. This philosophy can be used in any model.

MONTESSORI PHILOSOPHY

Montessori is child-centered, hands-on, real life context philosophy of education, which attempts to develop the whole child. When done as homeschool, can be a non-graded one room school.

POWER OF AN HOUR PHILOSOPHY

While the Power of an Hour is a homeschool curriculum created by Donna Goff, the philosophy behind it, is a hybrid of a cottage school, Leadership Education, Charlotte Mason, Principle Approach, and elements from Donna Goff. For more details on the Power of an Hour curriculum see Chapter Eight, under recommended resources.

RAYMOND MOORE PHILOSOPHY

Raymond Moore philosophy holds that both work and play are the foundation for academic learning and that formal academic learning should be delayed until eight or ten. Meanwhile they are developing their executive functions, core values, work ethic, and context for academic learning.

SPINE APPROACH

A spine is a book that you use as a road map through a subject. A spine and the internet or a library card would be all you need. A spine helps you to know what to cover. Then the internet or the library card helps you dig deeper and learn about the subject. This would be for basic history or basic skills. This philosophy can use any model of education.

WALDORF PHILOSOPHY

Waldorf is an individualized, integrated, child-centered holistic approach to learning. This integrates the child's imaginative, creative, intellectual, and practical learning.

Did any of these philosophies resonate with you? Which one and why?

DECIDING ON YOUR HOMESCHOOL METHOD

Once you have identified the various models and philosophies of education and you have decided on which one you like the best it is time to talk methods. In this section, we will break things down into the actual methods for how to apply your model and philosophy.

Keep this in mind. Many of these methods can be done together as a family, a student could be assigned to do them independently, or a student interested in a subject could use these methods. So, these methods can be applied to all three educational models.

Note: this is how you can take a curriculum that is not working for you and switch it up to fit your model and philosophy of choice.

BOOK OF CENTURIES

The Book of Centuries is a timeline in a book and was originally created by Charlotte Mason.

Donna Goff created a new updated Book of Centuries that has parallel timelines for each major of the continents. The index pages act as a table of contents for the content the student adds as they study.

BOOK OF NATIONS

The Book of Nations is an annotated Gazetteer. Here the student curates knowledge they have learned about different countries and then organizes them into an easy to access format. This was inspired by the book of centuries, but was created by Donna Goff.

You can learn more about Donna Goff's Book of Centuries and Nations in Chapter 8 where we discuss recommended Educational Resources.

CLASSICS, ANNOTATIONS, AND DISCUSSION

Classics, Annotations, and Discussion is a Leadership Education key method in the Leadership Education model. The young scholar reads a classic, annotates ideas in a notebook, and then discusses the book with others.

GREAT COURSES

Great Courses are classes done on video and some with work books. They get the best teachers to teach the subjects.

NATURE STUDIES

Nature Studies are a gateway to science. Charlotte Mason promoted nature studies and nature notebooks as a foundation of learning science. This is simply observing nature, making a record of what you see, and then doing the research to learn more, and label it properly.

NOTEBOOKING

Notebooking is used in the Noah Plan. In Notebooking, a children's classic, fiction, or nonfiction book, is used as the course. As they come to names mentioned, places mentioned, events mentioned, the student looks up and learns about those things and records them in their notebook. Students use 4Ring in their notebooking.

4RING - RESEARCH, REASON, RELATE, AND RECORD

Research is subject or word study. Reason is to recognize the main idea and the basic principles in the reading. Relate the main ideas and basic principles to other things they are studying, to the world around them and especially to themselves. Record their authentic learning and conclusions.

4Ring is from the Noah Plan. When students are studying a subject and dig deeper into understanding a subject, they use the four steps of learning, research, reason, relate, and then record what God is teaching them about the subject.

NARRATION

Narration is a Charlotte Mason learning device. Narrations can be either oral or written. The child recalls the details of what was just read to them. They get one pass.

Picture Studies is a Charlotte Mason way to study art. The children view the art then describe it from recall. This also builds attention to detail.

PROJECT BASED LEARNING

Project Based Learning is learning through projects. The project could be anything— creating a book on dinosaurs, putting on a play, making egg noodles, learning to play an instrument, planting a garden, or creating a home business.

This can be done as a family, a student could be assigned to do the courses independently, or a student interested in a subject could take the course. So this can fit all three models.

UNIT STUDIES

Unit Studies are studies focusing on learning in depth about one subject, but as you do, other skills are used. A unit study can be based on a children's classic, a topic like planets in our solar system, or studying about a state.

YOUTUBE

Youtube has videos on how to do just about anything, as well as documentaries, lectures, music lessons, and do-it-yourself videos. This site can be used as a family, a student could be assigned to do the learning videos independently, or a student interested in a subject could use Youtube for self-directed independent study.

So, this can fit all three models. Youtube can also be a reference resource.

So which method or methods listed above stood out to you? It is totally ok to utilize multiple methods in your homeschool to fit the needs of your family.

BUDGET: HOW DO I COVER THE COST OF HOMESCHOOL?

As we discussed earlier in this chapter homeschooling curriculums and supplies can be expensive. However, We would like to point out that Homeschooling can actually be more affordable than you might think. Especially when you teach family style and use mastery for skills.

Some curriculums may seem expensive if you are trying to purchase them all at once. However, you can often find them on sale or purchase them through a month to month plan making these large written curriculums more affordable on a budget.

It is also important to know that there are several great educational resources available that are completely free.

(We will be reviewing some of our favorite curriculums and resources in Chapter Eight so don't miss that section.)

The best way to budget your desired homeschool curriculums, resources and materials is to first make your list of what you really want. Next, prioritize your list. Lastly, it is important to be creative and think outside the box for how you can afford what you want.

Years ago, a friend decided to homeschool. She researched and created a list of what she wanted to use in her home. She added up the cost and it was simply outside her budget. So, she and her daughters started doing bake sales and looked for other ways to earn money over the summer. When they secured the amount to purchase her wish list, she ordered all of it at once. She said, it was like Christmas when the packages started arriving! Each day another parcel would arrive and her children gathered round to see what was inside. This built up excitement and value for what they were about to learn.

The children and the mother worked hard to make it happen. They were invested. It would not have been the same if she had put it on a credit card, drew it from savings, or found funds in other ways. Everyone was on "Team Mom" because everyone helped make it happen. Her attitude was to never tell the children, "We can't afford it." It was always, "Let's figure out how to make it happen!"

This attitude blessed her family over the years and her children developed a "Can Do" attitude. There simply was no such thing as outside the budget. She taught them how to think outside the box, make things happen and not go into debt.

Remember, when making your homeschool budget, you want to include funds for more than just purchasing curriculum. Consider budgeting for museum passes, fun educational field trips, tools like microscopes, globes, whiteboards, and of course good books as well as anything else you want to get for your homeschool.

HERE IS A BASIC STARTER LIST OF IDEAS OF WAYS TO EARN EXTRA MONEY TO FUND YOUR HOMESCHOOL

Do you need some ideas for how to earn extra money for your homeschool budget?

Here are some things your children can do, things you can do, and things you can all do together to earn that extra money you need to get those homeschool items on your wish list.

- Bake sales
- Yard care
- House sitting, checking mail, feed animals, water plants
- Take out and bring in garbage cans
- Car detailing
- Child care
- Dog walking
- House cleaning
- Website building
- Virtual Assistant
- Creating Graphic Design Files
- Teach classes on something you do well and like
- Grow flowers and learn flower arranging, sell arrangements
- Sell home crafted items online - soaps, herbed salts, t-shirts, home or garden decor, gifts, holiday decor, handmade items, even freezer meals, etc.

Just think outside the box. What can you do well?

One other suggestion, if any of the items you want are available on Amazon or sites that allow you to create wish lists, consider making a homeschool wish list for your family. Then if friends or family are trying to decide what to get for your family for special occasions or christmas they can refer to those lists. This is also a way for grandparents who want to be involved in their grandchildren's education to know what to get you.

Again, If you want recommendations for a specific curriculum, we will be covering that later in the book in Chapter 8: Recommended Resources.

4 SETTING UP THE "SCHOOL" PART OF YOUR HOMESCHOOL

Now that you know the legal requirements in your state for your homeschool. You have your homeschool business plan created or at least started. And you have found the homeschool model, philosophy and methods that resonate with you, *(and may have even chosen your actual curriculum)*.

It's now time for the fun part. It's time to actually set up the physical homeschool in your home!

Setting up the school part of your homeschool actually has two parts. The first is your branding which we will explain next. Then it's finally time to get your supplies and set up your homeschool learning area. I recommend getting your children involved in the process. Let them help you set up the school in your home so they can feel a claim to it.

BRANDING YOUR HOMESCHOOL

While technically creating a homeschool brand is not necessary, it is something we highly recommend. Though some might consider having a school name, logo, and motto as merely fun extras, there are actually solid reasons why you should consider having them.

CREATING YOUR OFFICIAL HOMESCHOOL NAME

Let's start by talking about a school name. Your school name is important to have when creating transcripts for your children when they want to apply to colleges or universities. So, make sure you choose a professional school name. For example, we chose Groves Academy vs Groves Family Home School or Hogwarts (yes my kids are huge Harry Potter fans) In some states, each homeschool is established, for the lack of a better term, as a small private school. This is another reason to have an official name for your homeschool.

CHOOSING YOUR HOMESCHOOL MOTTO

Next, let's talk about mottos. A motto is a short phrase or sentence that embodies the ideals or beliefs of an institution. Having a homeschool motto puts into words your "homeschool why" and vision. It reminds both you and your children the reason you are homeschooling, as well as what sort of homeschool you have. It also looks good on your homeschool letterhead which you should use for official papers.

DESIGNING YOUR HOMESCHOOL LOGO

A logo is the crown of your homeschool branding. When creating your homeschool logo keep in mind the colors, fonts, and images you use. Your logo can be as simple or complex as you desire but should tie in with your name and symbolically represent your homeschool.

Again you would use your Logo in conjunction with your school name and motto when you create your children's transcripts, as well as on any official paper correspondence made on behalf of your homeschool. Having a logo is also nice for creating student and teacher IDs and even shirts (for when you are on field trips) It makes everything more official looking.

While none of these are strictly vital for setting up your homeschool they are all good ideas to have and will come in handy. They can be fun to create together with your kids.

STUDENT & TEACHER ID CARDS

As a side note about creating Student and Teacher ID Cards: Many companies and places now accept homeschool parents as teachers offering teacher discounts and homeschool children as students for student discounts. However, they often require an ID and in some cases a copy of your homeschool affidavit or a letter on the official school letterhead to claim. Something to keep in mind.

SETTING UP YOUR HOMESCHOOL CLASSROOM

When it comes to setting up your homeschool classroom, it is easy to get caught up in the idea that you have to actually convert a room in your home to look like a traditional classroom.

Most people do not have a spare room so they have to commandeer their living room or dining room into this classroom, complete with desks, chalkboards and posters on the walls. While this works for some people it is not necessary or even in many cases the best option.

Personally, we are not a fan of setting up a classroom in our homes. For those who are like minded, we would encourage you to think outside the box. The following are some innovative alternatives to the standard classroom setup that still allow for organization and structure.

CONSIDER YOUR WORK AREAS

A Family Work Station
If you can, consider setting up a family work station with a computer, a good office chair and lighting. This is great for children to use for homeschool. For those with limited space who don't have a workstation, but intend to use online resources, we recommend investing in laptops and tablets that can be used at the dining table.

Using the Dining Room Table
We use our dining room table a lot in our homeschool. It is perfectly located near the kitchen sink for crafts or science projects. And again the table has ample space for multiple laptops, or when children are doing writing.

HAVE HOMESCHOOL RESOURCE STORAGE AREAS

Book Shelves
Having a dedicated homeschool bookshelves are not only great for storing books, but they are also great for storing school supplies in baskets, as well as specialty equipment on the top shelves, such as a globe, microscope, magnifying glass, laptops, and tablets.

A Morning Crate, Morning Basket, or Morning Tote
These storage options can be purchased for under $10. They are great to use your resources that you use for group teaching. Eventually, each child could have their own basket or box to put their library books in and projects. Again these can be stored on or next to your bookshelves.

An Ikea Cart
These metal utility carts can be an inexpensive storage option on wheels. You can get one for about $30. If you have elementary through high school aged children , these are great for art supplies, office supplies, materials for science experiments etc.

Since they are metal and have more than one basket shelf. Best of all, the top can serve as your morning basket.

INVEST IN HOME SCHOOL SUPPLIES

Hopefully you budgeted to take advantage of back to school sales for basic office and art supplies. We like to check back at the end of the season to see if there are any Back to School super sale discounts being offered. Then we purchase items for next year if the deals are sweet enough.

One year we were able to get a case of composition books for .05 a piece! So, it's always worth checking.

We recommend considering purchasing a smooth clipboard for each child. This can be used as a mini-writing and drawing desk.

Also, we have found it is nice to have a portable white board or boogie boards on hand for the kids to use. They are great for doing math or working out other school problems while saving you a lot on paper.

For those using online resources we would again recommend considering investing in inexpensive laptops, as well as tablets such as a Kindle fire for your children to use. You can often find used electronics for a good price and they also often go on sale.

UTILIZE YOUR HOME ENVIRONMENT TO YOUR ADVANTAGE

Is your home being used to its best advantage to promote a love of learning in your children? If not, it is never too late to change your home environment. Here are a few suggestions we have for making your home more inviting to your children to study and learn.

Family Library

Do you have a family library? If not, don't worry, you can start with just a library card or a device and an internet connection. Then you can begin to build your library one book and one shelf at a time. The books you begin to collect will become resources for your family. On that book shelf, have a copy of your core canon. Your core cannon is what you use as your measuring stick for truth that you and your family will judge all other works by. Often your core cannon is your scripture.

Let grandparents know you are gathering quality books. We have found books at second hand stores, yard sales, inherited books, bought new and used books on Amazon. We would also suggest creating an Amazon wish list! Do not worry yet, about how you will build a home library. Just consider what you would want in that library.

Some kinds of books to consider for your home library:

- Bible
- Family History (Family Stories)
- Faith Builders
- Children's Classics
- General Knowledge
- Classics
- Magazines and Periodicals
- Film Classics
- Musical Scores
- Musical Classics
- Audio Classics

Library Card

If you are not ready to build a home library just yet, don't worry, if you have a local library then your library card will work for now. In addition to books, many libraries have audio books, ebooks, videos, and artwork that can be borrowed.

Frame It Refrigerator Culture

If you are looking for an easy way to introduce your children to art, quotes or scripture consider framing them and putting them on the fridge. That way as your family walks by the fridge every day they are exposed to that art piece, quote or scripture.

We did this by creating special frames where we could switch out the art piece, quote or scripture each week. We made these reusable frames by buying Pre-cut Picture Mat for an 8 x 10 picture from the hobby lobby. Then on the back we attached a clear plastic sheet protector and four .75 inch (1.9 cm) round magnets. These frames can be totally affordable to make, especially, if you use a weekly 40% off coupon

Dining Table Geography

A fun way to do geography is to put a world map on your table covered in clear vinyl. Which you can place a nice table cloth over for when you want a more formal table setting.

We did not have the wall space for our maps and again didn't want to have a classroom atmosphere in our main living rooms. So we decided to put the map we were using on our table.

When we did this, we enjoyed having the map available to reference when studying History, Geography or Current Events. However, we were easily able to cover that map when we wanted a more formal look for our dining room.

The clear vinyl makes the dining table an easy to clean up crafting station too. For those who would love to make their own map table, we bought our maps at Costco during mid-summer. Then we covered it with a table cloth of clear vinyl the length of our dining table plus 16 inches (makes an 8 inch drop at each end of the table). We bought our vinyl at Walmart.

Learning Adventure Jar
This jar is filled with slips of paper with a [activity] listed on each piece of paper. When children [don't know] what to do, they get to pull out a piece of paper and do the activity that is on the paper. The jar is free, repurposed, or you can acquire a jar from a store sale, garage sale, second hand store, under $5.

Discovery Inspiration Boxes
These boxes are clear plastic and shoe box size or the next size up. Each box you assemble contains a different kind of activity: everything you need for origami, for calligraphy, a book, an audio book, a puzzle, game or activity. You can brainstorm with your children to decide on what to put in the boxes. This may be a way to integrate resources you may already have. These clear plastic lidded boxes are typically $2 - $4 depending on the size

THE WORLD CLASSROOM

Ultimately the world is your classroom so when setting up your homeschool classroom, take into consideration utilizing resources outside of your home. Consider getting memberships to local museums, zoos, and aquariums. (for you will go more often if you have a membership)

Also look up what historical sites or sites of interest are nearby to visit. These can be wonderful teaching opportunities. Lastly, look at local businesses to see if they do private tours, and find local people willing to share stories, skills and subjects of interest with your children.

BEYOND LOCAL - TRAVEL WITH YOUR CHILDREN

We have found that as homeschoolers while we are often homebodies we LOVE to travel. When traveling there are so many fun opportunities you can turn into an educational experience for your whole family. With historical sites, places of interest, museums, aquariums and more just waiting for your family to explore. When we are traveling to a different state or country we like to study about the place before we go.

For example: Growing up I remember traveling with my family across our vast continent from the midwest all the way to the West Coast. I was only 6 but I remember stopping and seeing the historic sites and places of interest along the way. We then took an eleven and a half hour flight to our new state, in the middle of the Pacific Ocean. Though that was decades ago, I still remember that adventure. I fell in love with history and travel!

When my two oldest boys graduated from high school we decided to travel across the United States to see places of interest, see natural wonders, visit relatives, and see historical sites. At the time we had six children from seventeen months to seventeen years old. How would we manage that? We were not rich. In fact, my husband's job had just ended. I presented my plan to my husband. We would camp across the USA! I would cook dinner and breakfast on a camp stove and make sandwiches for lunch. I told him we pay for gas and groceries anyway, it would just be a little more. I swayed him! We left on Memorial Day and returned home by mid July. .

We traveled east to the Midwest, dropped down to the Gulf of Mexico, down to Key West, up to Charleston, inland through the Smokies, through Cumberland Gap, to Monticello, to Washington DC, To Philadelphia, through New York,

Vermont, New Hampshire, and Maine, to the Bay of Fundy, Nova Scotia and to Cavendish, Prince Edward Island, to New Brunswick, then south through New England to Niagara Falls, across Ontario, Canada to Detroit, to Chicago, across the Great Plains, over the Rockies, and home. We had traveled over 12,000 miles in six weeks, camping in state parks and on beaches across the nation. We had only stayed in a hotel two nights the whole trip! We even drove past Disney World and no one cried. We had seen so much of our country and still had half our adventure before us. My children dubbed this Mom and Dad's Great Adventure, and an adventure it was!

Over the years we managed other Mom and Dad's Great Adventures taking shorter trips through the Heartland, the Pacific Northwest, Western National Parks, the Pacific Coast Highway, the Southwest, and even to Hawaii. We got to do this because we made sacrifices and planned. In the process of traveling with my children, we saw a lot of natural beauty, we learned a lot about this great land and also planted travel seeds in our children.

Two of my daughters have traveled beyond our shores to Europe. One son has worked all over the US and he took time to enjoy the sites and local culture. Another son was able to travel with his wife to Australia for his company, because he was willing to not fly first class. They too travel on a shoestring and make it happen.

A friend wanted to do some summer travel with her family. Travel was outside their budget. So they decided to plan the trip as a family, anyway. Then they took on an evening job as a family and cleaned a small two floor office building. They earned the money in no time and were off on their adventure! Travel is doable, even if you are not rich. With a few sacrifices and some hard work, your family can enjoy the educational and cultural benefits of occasional travel.

RECORD KEEPING

Record keeping is important, even if your state does not require recordkeeping. Good record can be used by you to evaluate your homeschool. Records also provide a paper trail of what you have been studying. When you come back from a trip or pick up homeschooling after an illness, your records will help you know where to jump in and get restarted. There are three kinds of records I suggest.

The Simple Family Record
This is a basic record kept daily by the homeschool parent. It is often just one page (that can be kept on your computer or notebook). This simple record consists: The date, a record of what was done/studied as a family, and a record listing what was taught done with each child individually.

Children's Independent Record
This record is kept by the homeschool parent, until the child is able to keep it for themselves. This Child Record includes: The date and what that child studied/learned for homeschool that day. This record can be multiple pages and can include what they read that day, projects they worked on and any independent learning they did.

Scholar Portfolio
The Scholar Portfolio is like the Children's Independent record. The difference is in the depth and the details. As children grow and move into more independent studies this record is filled with details of all they are studying, learning, and doing.

5 HOW TO ADDRESS SOCIALIZATION NEEDS

There is a huge stigma of homeschool kids being socially awkward and inept. This is why the first question most people ask when they discuss homeschooling is, "But what about the socialization?"

This stigma dates back decades ago when there were a few extreme homeschool parents who not only removed their children from public school, but also went as far as to completely isolate them from associating with anyone not strictly homeschooled. These kids were cut off from virtually everyone and rarely learned basic social skills.

Now we would contend that these children were socially awkward due to their home culture and would have been socially awkward even if they had stayed in public school.

However, because they were homeschooled and were under the skeptical microscope of the world they were put forth as what happens when a child is homeschooled. Since then, it has been shown that this is NOT the normal outcome of homeschooling. In fact, unless a homeschooled person informed you of the fact that they were homeschooled, you probably wouldn't know (except for how bright they are).

Studies have actually shown that in many cases homeschooled children have advanced social skills for they have learned their social skills in an environment with people of various ages and situations. Versus children in public school who learn their social skills in controlled environments with only children their own age.

However, for those still concerned about making sure their children obtain the needed social skills to be successful in life here are some ideas for how to make sure your homeschool children are adequately socialized.

TEACHING SOCIAL SKILLS IN THE HOME

The most important place to teach and learn correct social skills, no matter where your children go to school, will always be in your home.

It is here that you learn your first lessons of civility, to say please and thank you and the importance of acknowledging the efforts of others. It is in the home where you are given your first lessons of sharing, conflict resolution (with siblings), respect of elders and how to talk to people courteously.

When these lessons are not actively taught and reinforced at home, it doesn't matter how much your children socialize with others and they will still probably be socially inept.

CONNECTING WITH LOCAL HOMESCHOOLERS

When I was homeschooled in my youth, most of my friends went to public school. While we had fun together, often I would feel like the outsider in conversations that revolved around what was happening with my friends at school together. I also had to field a lot of questions and comments my friends had about homeschooling (many that they inherited from their parents who didn't agree with my parents decision to homeschool my siblings and I).

Because of this, even though I too encouraged my kids to make friends in our neighborhood and church (regardless of where they attend school). I knew it was important to provide opportunities for my children to be able to get together with homeschool friends, so they could just play and have fun with other kids who understood their homeschool life.

Thankfully the homeschool community has grown in the United States a lot over the last few decades. There are so many more homeschool families, communities and programs available than ever before. Homeschool families need never feel isolated. They just need to know where to look to connect with other homeschool families for support and social opportunities.

When looking for other homeschool families to connect with, Google and Facebook can be a great resource. You can find homeschool support groups in every state via Google and on Facebook and often even more local. If you do not find a group nearby, consider starting your own support group in your home.

While many groups in certain states require statements of faith among other educational requirements to join, we recommend not limiting yourself. Have an open group where all are welcome, for you will find the diversity is only to your benefit.

GETTING INVOLVED

Homeschool groups and communities can offer some great opportunities to your and your children. Both educationally and socially. The key to remember when delving into the world of homeschool groups and communities is to be involved, yet not over involved.

Let us explain. It is great to take advantage of the support and wonderful opportunities homeschool groups and communities can offer, but you don't want to be caught up with these activities taking over your life. If you are running from one thing to another you will become stretched too thin, and can easily lose your homeschool focus and center.

Be picky with what you choose to participate in. Don't try to do it all at one time. There will always be more opportunities, which you can do later on. Just remember there is a time and a season for everything. It's ok to say no for now but I would love to later.

Here are some activities and opportunities you can find within homeschool groups and communities:

PARK DAYS

We held Park Days on Friday after lunch. There was no obligation to come and it was "come if you can." If other families joined us, the children played and the adults talked. If no one comes, mom plays with her children. Park days are great because they were held in the afternoon and did not interfere with our homeschool day. Also, there was no preparation, so they did not take time away from homeschool.

CO-OPS

Some people like co-ops. The upside is that there are children and moms to socialize with. There are some co-ops that operate like a private school. Some co-ops offer extra curricular specialty classes. Most meet once a week. But, some meet every day. The downside of co-ops is that they are a co-operative effort and they often have preparations that either the mother or the students have to do at home.

If a child is taking several classes and has a lot of preparation, the coop commitment can reach into your homeschool. Then soon, co-op becomes all that you do. If you do choose to participate in a coop, be careful and use your better judgment to make sure it doesn't take over your homeschool life.

FIELD TRIPS

Many places (like museums, zoos, aquariums, or special educational venues) offer group discounts for field trips. So, getting together a group of homeschoolers can save you money. Some venues will even offer homeschool days with free admission, if there is a big enough homeschool community in your area.

Our state zoo offers four FREE Homeschool days a year during the off season which we love to enjoy as a family.

MICRO CLASSES

A Micro Class is a short one or two day special interest class. It could be something as simple as how to do a square foot garden, parliamentary procedure, an astronomy class night under the stars, how to start a nature notebook when you are just learning to draw, short classes on a topic, make and take classes, such as, soap making or bread baking.

These micro classes are not about hiring someone to take over teaching a science or math class, week after week. These classes are meant to be short, one or two day classes of about three hours each day.

BOOK GROUPS

Homeschoolers like to read as well as listen to audio books. Book groups are not only great for helping you and your kids break down what you have learned and read in the books you are reading. They are also a fun way to get to know other homeschoolers in your area.

You can make a book group for children, youth or adults. Some do a book a month and meet together once a month to discuss the book. Others discuss the book and then watch a movie based on the book. Some book groups are themed and explore a specific genre. Others change it up and do short classics under 100 pages. Some do themed parties to celebrate the book with food, activities, and music tied to the theme, location, or time period of the book.

We had a mother-daughter Liber-tea Luncheon every month. Mothers and daughters read a book together each month. The classic children's book always exemplified a principle of inner beauty or outward grace to help us become better women. Then we would all meet for a book discussion over a potluck luncheon and we would do a humanitarian service or learn a home arts skill.

I held a book group with my younger two teen sons and other teen boys. We studied the Hobbit, Lord of the Rings Trilogy, Sun Tzu's Art of War, The Story of Liberty, and writings of C. S. Lewis. After the book group while the boys waited for their parents to pick them up, we had refreshments and they played games of stratagem.

Book groups can be fun, enriching, and be positive socialization as our youth learn how to discuss ideas with others who may see things differently, and still be respectful and be friends.

PARTIES

Parties are fun ways to get together with other homeschoolers to just have fun. When my children first started homeschooling, they felt deprived that they wouldn't have the traditional holiday parties that their friends would all talk about having at school (like for valentines day, Halloween and Christmas etc). So, we got together with a bunch of other homeschool families to do homeschool holiday parties and boy did we have fun.

Other homeschool parties can be dances, family balls (inspired by Jane Austen), proms, graduations or even parties "just because," such as skating parties, movie nights or game nights.

PLAYS, RECITALS AND SPELLING BEES

Getting together with other homeschool families makes it possible to do certain activities that would be difficult if not impossible to do on a smaller, family scale. Some ideas are plays and musicals. My grandsons in Colorado just did a *Midsummer's Night Dream* with their homeschool group. They streamed it online so families far away could enjoy it too. We had a group of homeschool violinists that joined with public school violinists in our neighborhood. The six girls put on a Sunday afternoon concert for the neighborhood on the front lawn of one of the families.

Concerts and recitals can include group numbers and solo performances, making this kind of activity easier to prepare for. Talent shows and art shows can be done in a park, in someone's yard or at a church. Since individuals are bringing their own creations these kinds of social activities are easy to prepare for. Lastly, there are competitive social activities such as, spelling bees, geography bees, science fairs, and debate. These are opportunities for children to show off what they have learned.

Thanks to the growing world of homeschooling worrying about socialization is a thing of the past.

6 ESTABLISHING A HOME CULTURE FOR LEARNING

What is home culture? Quite simply, home culture is the cultural atmosphere of the home. This atmosphere is where you nurture a love of cultural breadth and depth of knowledge in your family. It is where you cultivate work habits, routines and traditions to strengthen your family and give your children a solid foundation for learning. Your home is your household, its internal environment, and atmosphere. Culture means to cultivate.

So, home culture is the culture you cultivate in your home. What will the culture be like in your family? What activities, family traditions, and materials will you have in your home, to assist your family in becoming refined and cultured?

Many moms struggle with homeschooling because they have not considered how their home culture is impacting their homeschool and their children's learning. To be fair, many children that attend public, private and charter schools who struggle with learning struggle because of a lack of a strong home culture. Their teachers can all tell which children come from homes with a strong home culture and which do not.

In this chapter, we will discuss six areas that when we pay attention to them, can make all of the difference in our homeschooling and in our homes, in general. Again, these areas can impact your children whether they school at home, attend public school, a charter school, or attend a private school. When these areas are attended to, there can be less stress and more focus for learning.

Parents who struggle with their own habits and struggle with domestic work avoidance themselves, may also struggle in helping their children gain good habits and good work attitudes. So, in parenting and child training, it is helpful to first address our own issues before we look to address these issues with our children.

ASSESSING WHERE YOU ARE

It is time to assess where you are when it comes to work habits and attitudes by asking yourself some key questions: How are our habits?

How are our attitudes towards caring for the home? We all have to have a place to live and care for it, whether we have a family or not. Caring for our home is not something that only stay-at-home moms need to do. This work may be repetitive, but most work is.

Work brings us joy and opportunities. We love clean, fresh smelling clothes. So, we launder them. We love eating off of clean plates, using clean utensils, and sitting at a clean table, so we do dishes and wipe the table. We love walking across a clean floor that does not crunch or stick to our feet, so we clean the floor. Work brings blessings. When we focus on the blessings, it is easier to learn to love to do work. If work is worth doing it is worth doing well. We will discuss the how in the next chapter.

WORK ETHIC

Your work ethic will affect your success in every aspect of your life, not just education. This is one of the first foundational things parents need to teach their children at home no matter where they go to school. Work ethic isn't just knowing how to work, it is your attitude towards work itself. So, how do we teach our children to have a good work ethic?

When we work with our children, we are setting the pace for them and helping them learn how to pace themselves. We are also showing them our standard, helping them pay attention to the details, and helping them reach our standard. Just showing them once or even a few times is not enough. If we work systematically and do it the same way each time, we help them set a pattern. Those patterns, over time, become habits. Habits can be built into routines.

Again, work ethic isn't just about knowing how to work it's also about attitude.

So, as we work with our children we need to pay attention to our expressed attitude toward the work we are doing. We need to show them the value of doing hard work and not so fun things with a good perspective.

For example: Inviting children to work with you, with an invitation of, "I don't like this any more than you do, but it has to be done," does not value work or help them have good attitudes towards work. Rather, consider saying to your children, "I know this is hard, but we can do hard things, if we sing and work hard, we will feel the reward of a job well done."

DEVELOPING PERSONAL HABITS

We all recognize the fact that our children need to be trained to walk, talk, listen, use the toilet properly, wash their hands thoroughly, brush their teeth, drink from a cup, eat with utensils, and get dressed. Those core basic habits are vital. However, it is important to not stop here. There are other important habits that we need to help our children develop for successful learning and life.

It is common to fall into the mindset that once our children begin talking, that they all the sudden fully understand what we want them to do in every circumstance and are mature enough to just do it. And so we stop focusing on continuing to train our children in those habits and switch to just assigning work. This can lead to lots of frustration and stress for both the parents and the children.

Parents in these circumstances find themselves disappointed and frustrated when assigning is not enough to get the work done. Some parents resort to visual check off lists with pictures and while that may work for some children, it does not work for others. This disconnect has something to do with child executive function development. It takes a child more than knowing what you want done and how to do it. Researchers in child development have found that often, the expression of intellect, the senses, and the child's development, rarely track together. Meaning, if you are high in intellect, such as an early reader or math whiz, it does not mean your sensory development and your executive function development have reached the same level. Sensory integration is a topic for another book.

EXECUTIVE FUNCTION

Since Executive Function is a key element in developing personal habits, let us talk a bit more about executive function. What is executive function development? Executive Function is our internal CEO, a set of cognitive and organizational skills that are developed after birth and throughout childhood. Executive functions include skills, such as-- attention span, organizational skills, working memory, the ability to set a goal, pay attention to detail, control impulses, delay gratification, emotional self-regulation, follow-through, finishing, and organizational skills. There are more, this was just a brief list. These are developed after birth, throughout life, are not automatic with age and as previously noted, are not necessarily more developed in children with higher IQs.

Self-directed play, both imaginative play and varied outdoor activities can improve and develop both sensory development and integration, as well as executive function development.

Just a note: On the physical sensory development side, because even this can impact executive function development. Outdoor activities help development and later help academics. Activities such as crawling, walking, running, dancing, jumping, sliding, swinging, spinning, rolling, brachiating, balancing, skating, sliding, bouncing, and more, help develop and integrate the senses. They also help lay the foundation for both academic and executive function development.

Sensory development and executive function is why many professionals encourage delayed academics. These are vital foundational pre-academic areas that need to be developed FIRST. They become the foundation and scaffolding to build upon. We would not consider building a building without proper foundations and internal structure. We recommend taking time to address both sensory and executive function development.

Some wonder why can't we do both? It is because, usually, once the academics begin, these areas tend to take the back seat, and are valued less. And it can take a while to realize how vital these areas are. This usually shows up in problems with cooperation, learning and developing work ethic.

How does executive function impact learning how to work, fulfill expectations and develop personal habits?

Let us use this example: Your child hears you ask them to clean their room. They either lose it (whining, complaining and sometimes full out tantrums over the request), or they head to their room to comply. If the child loses it, this can be an indication that their executive function development has a way to go on emotional self-regulation. If the child is doing something and does not want to leave it to do what you ask, they may be struggling with delaying gratification. This could also be an opportunity for a parent to consider timing of requests. If your child goes to their room and begins to work, but then ends up playing, they may struggle with impulse control, delayed gratification, or it may even indicate that they lack the organizational skills needed, causing them to just zone out.

What about the three year old or even seven year old that has learned to read, but has a tantrum and plays instead of cleaning? You need to keep in perspective that they are probably not consciously deciding, "How can I make mom miserable?" In reality, they may just not be ready for solo work. They may be struggling with self-regulation development, impulse control, may also lack follow through skills or may lack organizational skills. This is where habit training can help a lot, while those executive functions are developing.

HABIT TRAINING

Let's discuss habit training. What is habit training? How does it work? Why is it important? Habit training begins with you leading by example, walking beside your children, and helping them until the pattern is set.

Personal habits take practice, a lot of practice. However, it is worth it. For, when we fail to develop and teach good habits in our home, we sacrifice future peace and sanity for present convenience.

To help your children develop these habits, it will take regularly doing them with your children until the habits are solid. While the task may take moments, having the pattern set as a habit takes time. Helping your children to form important habits can often take longer than we think. This is because many of us have poor habits ourselves that we need to fix first. Mom's habits are part of mom care in the next chapter so we won't discuss them here.

While some children tend to take longer than others, it is important to note that most girls tend to develop faster than most boys (usually by about two years) So, be patient with them as they grow. Be kind in your guidance. Be consistent in promoting the development of those regular personal habits.

One habit we recommend cultivating with your children that will make life easier for everyone is to teach your children to pick up after themselves as they go along, rather than waiting until there are lots of little messes to clean up.

When children are taught to pick up immediately before going to do something else, there will be fewer messes to deal with.

Sure they can stop and run to the potty if needful, but then it is back to put away what they were using. If you will take the time to do this they will need fewer routines.

When we take care of things immediately, they stay in better repair, last longer, and thus save us money. They also save us time later, as we won't have to wade through messes and figure where to start to tackle the messes.

Here are a few other specific habits that we recommend focusing on with your children to make your home and homeschool life run smoother:

- When you are teaching your children to fold clothes, make sure to teach them to put those clean clothes away as soon as they are folded. If necessary, walk your children to their room and watch them put their clothes away properly. (not just randomly stuffing them into drawers.) Yes, this is a habit that many moms confess to struggle with. If you are one of those, don't worry, just work on developing it with your children.

- When you are teaching your children to bathe, make sure to teach them also how to clean up their bathtime mess afterwards (dirty clothes, towels, bath toys etc) and if necessary help them to do it.

- When you teach your children to dress for bed, make sure you teach them that dirty clothes come off the body and go into the hamper, and have them do it. Remind your children that dirty clothes do not belong on the floor, on the bed or stuffed behind pillows.

- When you are teaching your children to brush their teeth, make sure to teach them to put the toothbrush and toothpaste away afterwards. Also teach them that if they made a mess on the counter or in the sink, how to properly clean it up and have them do it.

- When you are reading books to your children or letting them handle books, make sure to teach them to put the books back on the shelf when they are finished reading or looking at them.

- When your children play with their toys or games, make sure to teach them to put the toys or games away when they are done. They need to do this before they go to play with something or someone else. It is also important to teach your children to take the time to clean up toys and games they play at friends' or families' homes, before they leave.

- When your children are big enough to sit at the table and not in a high chair, make sure to teach them how to clear their dirty dishes when they are done eating and take them to be rinsed and stacked (if not loaded into the dishwasher).

- If your children have an accident of any kind, then help them learn how to clean it up! Don't just do it yourself to save time.

- When your children get up in the morning, help them learn to make their own bed. Don't just do it yourself. Rather, help them do it so that they can gain the habit. If you live in a dry climate, your children can make their beds immediately. If you live in a damp climate, teach them to pull down the covers and let their beds air out during breakfast, and then help them form the habit to make their beds right after breakfast.

- If your children are playing with toys, balls, bikes, scooters, outside, make sure to teach them to put their outside toys away before coming inside. This way things are less likely to be weather damaged, run over, or stolen.

CHILDREN'S ROUTINES

Routines are a series of habits linked together. So, routines are built on habit training. They are the next step. Sometimes parents make the error of seeing a series of actions, as a single action, when really there are several steps involved.

When considering routines consider ones for in your home and ones for when visiting elsewhere. The following are two examples of routines built on habits of putting things away. The first would be an example of these clean up routines when visiting someone. The second example is of a cleanup routine at home.

We have a friend with grown children and young grandchildren. She has a simple routine when her grandchildren come over. She has a big rug in the family room and a toy box. Grandchildren visit and know they can bring out the toys and play on the huge area rug. However, when they are done playing before they go home, her grandchildren are expected to put all the toys away in their proper basket.

As a young mom, I (Donna) was often frustrated. My two oldest children are very bright. They taught themselves how to read at the same time, when the oldest was four and the younger was two. This happened when I was expecting my third child.

Because of how bright they were, I thought that even though I had not trained them in habits they knew what I wanted and how to do it. So, I would tell them to go clean their room. However, instead of cleaning their room, they would often end up just playing.

I learned that even though my boys were bright, they still needed me there guiding them while they matured. Cleaning their room was a huge task. No, it was a group of tasks and subroutines to clean a bedroom.

There is a systematic way to clean a room. If your children are not yet independent cleaners, they need to be trained to do it properly. Consider cleaning their room is your routine and your children are your apprentices. Grab their hands and say, "Let's clean your room together."

If you need help developing this routine, you can print off the list below to help. Use this list with your children, so you can do it with them in the same pattern each time. When your children are older and more experienced, they can do it their own way, it won't matter as long as it is all done.

However, before your children are independent, don't just do the cleaning yourself. Even toddlers can help and learn. Again, you can print off the steps below and use the lists as your road map, or you can make your own list. Just be clear, consistent and do things in the same order each time to help your children form those patterns into habits and routines.

---

1. MAKE THE BED

Oops, that is actually a routine!

- Clear the bed.
- Tuck in the sheet.
- Pull up the sheet and smooth the sheet.

- Pull up the blanket.

- Fold the pajamas and place them under the pillow.

- Fluff the pillow and put it at the head of the bed, over the pajamas.

- Cover with bedspread.

Now you have a clean and clear surface to use as a staging area for the rest of the room if needed. Of course, if this is a habit to do first thing in the morning, it does not have to be part of a bedroom cleaning routine, because it is already done.

2. LAUNDRY

Oops, another subroutine.

Sometimes, folded clothes are brought to the room, but not put away. They can end up on the floor and then into the hamper. So, it is important to teach them how to sort and what to do with the clothes.

- Sort clean from dirty clothes.

- Are there any clothes needing to be put away? Where do they go? Drawer or closet?

- Grab hangers, hang clothes needing hanging, and place them in the closet.

- Fold clothes, if they need folding, and place in drawers. Even preschool aged children can learn to fold.

- Place dirty clothes in the hamper.

Of course, if clothes are properly put away when clean and the habit of placing dirty clothes into the hamper is established, this won't need to be part of the bedroom cleaning routine.

More subroutines. If children are habit trained, these issues are rare.

3. BOOKS

- Place Books on the shelf.

- What if they are reading a book and want to do something else? Have them bookmark the page and then place on the shelf, desk, or nightstand to finish later. Books should never be left on the floor when not in use!

Of course, if books are properly put away while not in use, this does not have to be part of a bedroom cleaning routine.

4. BELONGINGS

- Pick up any other belongings and put them away.

Of course, if belongings are put away when not in use, they do not have to be part of a bedroom cleaning routine, because they are not part of the mess.

5. GAMES

- Put game pieces in their boxes.
- Place games boxes on the shelf.

Of course, if games are put away when they are finished, this does not have to be part of cleaning the bedroom either.

6. TOYS

- Put toys back in containers.
- Place containers on the shelf.
- Pick up toys that go on the shelf and place on the shelf.
- Pick up toys that go in a toy box

Of course, if children are trained to put away toys that are no longer being played with, this won't be part of a routine either.

As we had more children, our children received birthday and Christmas presents, we ended up moving their games and toys from their rooms, and stored them in a game closet. Their games were stored on the shelves. Their toys were divided into clear plastic stackable containers.

The containers were stacked in the bottom of the closet. So, now to put the toys away, they needed to sort the toys first. We trained them that everything still had a proper place.

- A large container for legos

- A large container of building blocks
- A large container of dress ups
- A small container of cars and trucks
- A small container of dolls

As you can see there are many steps to cleaning a bedroom! If a child is not yet doing multi-step arithmetic, they will probably struggle to remember all these steps. Even if they have a list to go by, every toy or possession they pick up is an invitation to distraction, especially for a child that is still developing impulse control, delayed gratification, follow through, and finishing.

Habit training each routine will help your children, through giving them patterns and repetition to become part of them. Better yet, teach them habits first and fewer routines are needed.

We recommend fewer toys and fewer screen opportunities. We are not suggesting eliminating toys or screens. We are merely recommending you review how many and what you have. Then see if you could or should let go of some.

Too many things for a child or an adult to manage, can be overwhelming. Rather be selective with what you have. Less can be more. We have found that when our children had fewer toys, they tended to play with them more and they took better care of them. Which is why we implemented a rule in our that when our children get new toys they let go of older ones.

You could also rotate what toys you have out of storage, so they only have a certain number available at any given time to play with.

It is also important to note that screens can be an issue with young children. They can lead to building impulse reactions. We want them to learn to control impulse when they need to and be quick when they need to. So, if this is something your children struggle with, consider limiting screen time more, while placing an emphasis on screen free play.

Habits and personal routines can take time to establish, but once established you will be glad you did! Once a habit is fully formed your children will do it without constant reminders.

CHORES / FAMILY WORK

A big area of concern for parents, especially homeschool parents is trying to figure out how to balance keeping their home clean and orderly, while at the same time homeschooling their children.

CHORES

To address this need, many parents have resorted to creating set chores that they introduce to their children at specific ages. These chores are created to keep the house clean without mom having to do everything. This makes sense...right?

Sadly, the truth is, that while chores work well for many families, many other families struggle with implementing chores in their home. These parents often find themselves jumping from one chore system to another hoping that this one will work better. Yet, these parents still struggle to get their children to do their chores independently, even when they are supposedly age appropriate.

Note: *There are a lot of chore charts and systems available out there that have worked for the families that created them. Just be aware that when it comes to age appropriate charts, children the same age are not always at the same stage of development.*

That's when rewards or bribes come into play. Some parents have seen results with offering incentives for their children to do their assigned chores, while others find themselves constantly increasing what they are offering their children in order to get them to do the same amount of work. So what is the answer?

FAMILY WORK

As an alternative to individual chores, we would like to explore another option that we have found works. To be clear, we started out doing chores and did so for fifteen years in our family. As our younger children were coming into the system, it became apparent that the chore system was no longer working in our family. We tried several ways of tweaking chores, but they just were not working. At this time we came across the concept of "Family Work".

We discovered that family work is how families in America worked before factory efficiency experts suggested that the home follow the factory model. In talking to many who were raised prior to World War II, we discovered that most did family work. Children would work together in the home, along with mom, to get things done. When they were big enough to work outside they would take their work ethic and go outside to help dad. The perfect example of this was a book by Pearl S. Buck, *Christmas Day in the Morning*.

So, what exactly is family work? Family work is work shared between parents and children working shoulder to shoulder together, assisting each other. These tasks lend themselves to family work: preparing meals, setting the table, clearing the table after meals, doing the dishes after meals, sorting laundry, folding laundry, general tidying, general dusting, yard work, detailing and washing the car.

When can children join in family work? Once children are toddlers, most children do try to pitch in and help. Let them! When I (Donna) was expecting my second child, I would sit on the floor with my oldest son and sort laundry. I said what I was doing as I did it and he joined in-- Lights, darks, whites, towels, and dress clothes. He got very good at sorting and he was not even two years old.

The crazy thing is that when my oldest children were seven, five, and three, I abandoned something that was working for us, family work. I replaced it with chores. Why? Because that is what I thought all good parents did. We even got into those common escalations that I refer to as the *chore wars*. A chore war is when a parent gives an incentive and the incentive no longer works. The parent can increase the incentive or they can turn to threats of lost privileges. Eventually, neither may work. I wanted my children to find joy in work because they will have work to do the rest of their lives. They might as well make peace with it now.

So, what made me change back to family work? Perspective. I belong to a mother's book group. We had read *Sidetracked Home Executives*, and I had just completed the file system of our home. When I went back to report to the book group that I was finished, a lady offered an article to us on family work. The concept blew my mind.

That night I went home and I watched my six year old son load the dishes in the dishwasher. It was his chore that week. Everyone else disappeared and were doing their own thing. That night I was observing. My heart was open. I watched him solemnly and methodically load the dishes. He worked slowly and consistently. He was not dilly dallying. I sensed a deep feeling of abandonment. So, immediately I repeated what I had to older children before, "Son, I know this is hard, but next week you will be on trash and that is a lighter chore." This time, those words sounded hollow to me. He was in the moment and I unvalidated his feelings as I tried to distract and cheer him. I got up and helped him finish.

After we loaded the dishwasher, I called a family meeting. I didn't even warn my husband. I grabbed the chore chart and dramatically tore it to shreds. I know they wondered if I had lost my mind. I then told them we would not be doing chores anymore. I almost chuckled as they exchanged puzzled glances. Then I told them, we would now be doing family work. Then I explained what family work is.

Family work is great for adult children at home too. A friend had a huge home and family business. Some of her adult children moved home to help in the family business. They tried assignments, but somehow the youngest adult ended up doing all the work. My friend asked what to do. I suggested family work. No one gets stuck working in the kitchen alone, while everyone else skips out to be entertained or to do their own thing. Everyone began to work together and began to feel closer together, through family work.

Over the years we have recommended family work to other parents struggling with making chores work and like me they had amazing results in their home.

What about chores like bathrooms, cleaning the fridge, and other important skills, where the family cannot all fit in the room?

APPRENTICESHIP

The next step after chores or family work is apprentice. As I thought about teaching children how to work, I wanted to do more than just assign a few token chores. I came to see that teaching children to work is more about preparing them for a whole life, than just dividing labor. I looked around at moms I was working with, many struggled with running a home and I wanted to make sure my children could run a home. One brilliant mom, who had prepared herself to go to medical school said, "My mom taught me to clean a toilet, a tub, sinks, do laundry, but I had no idea how to orchestrate them into a system."

I decided the best way to teach these skills is to do it with them. Most moms that assign chores, give out a few chores to each child and then reserve the rest for themselves. Eventually, they might teach their children how to do things, but they never get to the point of having a system or life patterns to take with them when they grow up. When they leave home and start their own home, whether they are single or married, domestic work can tend to pile up, until they have no choice but to do it. I wanted to help my children to start adult life with confidence.

When children are about eight, they are bigger and stronger, this is the perfect time to apprentice them to you. They become your shadow and helper, helping you in all you do to run the home. They help with menu planning, shopping for food, and preparing meals with you. They help you with deep cleaning. Your children help you with those jobs that do not lend themselves to family work due to cramped spaces. This is a time for them to see how you budget! If you have more than one child over eight, switch it up and rotate with them. If children apprentice until they are a teen, they will know how to run a home, top to bottom and inside out. They will also know the importance of and how to budget.

By the mid teen years, most children have enough executive function development that they begin to take the initiative. This is usually after puberty. Also, children with good habits, lots of experience with teamwork through family work, and a solid background in helping you run the home. By this time they are trained enough to be able to take responsibility for one of the home systems, such as lawn care, laundry, or meal planning, shopping, meal prep. They can even orchestrate siblings helping them.

FAMILY ROUTINES

In times past, children grew up in homes that had family routines. When they left their homes to start their own, they took those routines with them. Most of us are familiar with

Monday is wash day,
Tuesday is ironing day,
Wednesday is sewing day,
Thursday is market day
Friday is cleaning day
Saturday is baking day

Those routines may not work for many of us today, but they were used to illustrate a point. If the list does not work for you, observe your family and make your own list. For instance, most clothes today are no-iron clothes. So, most of us do not need an ironing day, unless we like and want a crisp look. We can also see why many stores still put out ads to begin on Thursday!

We now live in the 21st century and many of us grew up in homes that did not have set routines because our mothers worked. So, what kind of family routines will help modern homeschool families? We still need to shop for food, make meals, clean them up, need to do laundry, yard care, a tidy house, and deep cleaning.

SHOPPING FOR FOOD

When my children were apprentice aged, I actually took them shopping with me. I wanted them to know how to select good

The best way to learn is in the trenches. I let them know they were there to learn and not to beg. If they did not behave we left. I create a menu and I consult the ads, and prefer shopping Friday afternoon after the school week.

I only bought meat on sale. I would talk to my children about the different products and why I chose the size I did. I wanted them to learn how to think economically when shopping.

I even went so far as to reading "The Grocery Store Game" by Janine Bolon, to my children. Janine went over how stores use psychology in how they place foods in the store. Right after finishing the book, I took them shopping. It was really funny, every time they started to ask for something, then stopped themselves in their tracks, because they remembered what Janine said in the book! As adults, they are frugal and live well.

MEAL PREP

Children can be taught how to do meal prep. We like to meal prep in the morning. Salad dressings can be made in the morning and have all day for seasoning to blend together. Children can be taught how to make salads. We chop, rinse, and spin romaine in the morning. We can tightly pack two prepared romaine heads, into a wide mouth quart jar. It comes out of the jar crisp at dinner.

Take time to check the menu in the morning or the night before, locate the ingredients, including from the freezer, and bring to the kitchen. When meals are prepared in the morning, or night before, getting dinner on the table at a regular time each evening.

MEAL CLEAN UP

Clean up after meals with your family. This includes, wiping all surfaces, sweeping the floors, putting away food and condiments. This leaves the dining table available for family games, learning, and also is prepared for a bright start in the morning.

Also, when family members do extra balking, we have three rules:

1. Start with a clean kitchen. Because if children start with a mess, they are more likely to add to the mess. So, sometimes they have to clean up before they start.

2. If they are making something to take to share at an event outside the home, they need to make enough to leave some to share with our family. After all, we got to smell it baking! We want some!

3. Leave no trace. When they are done they need to put everything away, clean all the equipment used to make the treat, and wipe all the surfaces.

Nothing can be more overwhelming than walking into the kitchen to prepare a meal or use the dining table, than to find a mess that must be cleaned before we can make the meal or work at the table.

LAUNDRY

Some families teach each child to do their own laundry. With seven children and two parents that can be a logistical nightmare. It can be costly in terms of laundry soap and power to do laundry, too. So, we sort together and fold together. I run underthings and towels through on a sanitize cycle and that can take three hours. So, I throw in a load to wash while we sleep. After breakfast, one of us switches the load and starts another load. Once laundry is in motion in the morning it needs to be kept in motion. Set the timer. When it goes off, change the load. Set the timer for the dryer. When It goes off, have a few minute folding party. Then, see the children to their rooms and make sure the clothes get put away properly.

The rule during the day, once in motion, laundry is in motion until it is put away. Running laundry in the morning after breakfast, means laundry is being done while we do dinner prep and homeschool.

YARD CARE

Yard care can be worked into the family routine. Many hands can make the work light. Just fifteen minutes a day is all that is needed.

We have a family friend that grew up in South East Asia. She was a member of the extended Royal Family. She said that her father had her and her siblings working the garden each morning before going to school. Even being part of the Royal Family, they were not above the work!

TIDYING

When we first began to homeschool, we tidied after breakfast because I simply could not focus to teach in a mess. I found it was taking too much of my morning. So, I switched tidying to after dinner in the evening, before bed. It only takes a few minutes if we work together. Then all we had to do in the morning was make our beds and clean up after breakfast. This made all the difference.

DEEP CLEANING

We have found that deep cleaning is best done with apprentices. We tidy a room. Then we clean from top down and from inside out. So, there is no stuffing clutter under the couch or inside cupboards.

LIFE SKILLS

It is best for children to learn life skills in the context of everyday life. Some things, such as canning and dehydrating food, we did as a family assembly line style. Other life skills are best learned one-on-one as they need to be done, such as fixing things around the house or replacing a flat tire on a car. When these circumstances arise, we advise you to take the time to teach your children what you are doing, even if it takes more time and energy. This way they can develop those skills.

BEDTIME ROUTINES

A bedtime routine is packed with many subroutines and habits:

- Tidy house and put toys away before bed, because it is nice to wake to a tidy house.

- Bathe because a clean body sleeps better.

- Dress for bed.

- Brush teeth. Bruising your teeth may seem simple, but it requires you to get the toothbrush, wet it, add toothpaste, and then properly brushing the gums, the teeth surfaces, and flossing in between.

- Use the toilet.

- Prayers

- Bedtime story, lullaby, or connection. Bedtime is the perfect time to connect one-on-one.

The bedtime routine may become a routine, if repeated regularly. But start with the individual habits. Get consistent and this repetition will help establish the habits into a routine.

MORNING CAN ALSO HAVE ROUTINES.

- Get dressed and put PJs away.

- Make bed.

- Eat Breakfast and clean up after breakfast.

- Brush teeth.

- Start homeschool.

Having a consistent routine is calming for children because they know what to expect. Knowing what to expect is a safer place, less stressful. Children with special needs tend to thrive in routines, too.

I found that when I just sent my kids to bed, after getting them in pajamas and their teeth brushed, they would still be up hours later after several "Go back to bed." speeches from me. However, if I prayed with them, sang two or three songs then read for thirty minutes to an hour from our current novel, then my kids would be out cold within minutes of me putting away the book. So, I now start our bedtime routine earlier and now have my evenings open to spend time with my spouse, get work done uninterrupted and even sneak in some me time.

SERVICE

Children need to know that the world does not revolve around them and that they can alleviate the suffering of others. Heck, most adults still need to learn this lesson. By Involving your children in thoughtful service opportunities it will help them to become compassionate and develop empathy for others.

These service projects can come in many shapes and sizes from writing thank you cards to doing food drives. From helping the elderly with their yard to taking a meal to someone who just had a baby.

A friend was using our Power of an Hour curriculum. Her children were three through fifteen. While she read aloud to her children, she kept their hands busy and they were able to listen and learn better. She taught them how to hat loom and even the youngest could. They made about thirty hats for the homeless shelter that fall.

FAMILY TIME

An important aspect of your home culture is your family time. We are serious when we state that family time is indeed sacred time. It is the time and activities you share together with your family on a regular basis. This is the time to strengthen your family unit as you help each other to build and develop their individual characters.

Below are a few family time activities that we recommend taking the time for with your spouse and children:

MEALTIMES

Family mealtimes are a great way to strengthen your family. While families having a sit down meal used to be an American institution, this tradition has become extinct in many busy American homes. We are so often rushing from event to event that grabbing food on the go has become a norm.

Coming together as a family each day for at least one meal, gives your family the opportunity to check in, enjoy delicious home cooked food and TALK. This is the time to talk about your day, what you are working on, what you are struggling with, current events and more. It is a time for bonding.

According to a recent study a few of the benefits of having a regular family dinners are:

- A lower risk of depression

- A lower risk of substance abuse
- Higher self-esteem
- A lower risk of teen pregnancy
- Better academic performance
- A lower likelihood of developing eating disorders
- Lower rates of obesity.

Thankfully, one of the blessings of homeschooling is you are home. So finding time for at least one sit down meal as a family every day is a whole lot easier. A few suggestions for making the most of your family meal time, especially if that meal is dinner:

- Have a rule that when dinner is ready, everyone has to stop what they are doing and come eat.
- Have your kids help you make the meal or at least set the table.
- Have a rule of no toys at the dinner table.
- Have a rule of no electronics at the dinner table (that means NO phones, NO tablets, NO headphones or earbuds and especially NO TVs)
- Take the time to ask each person about their day.

Note: When asking kids about school, don't ask a general question about what they learned that day. If you do so, you will most likely get the, "I don't know." response. Rather, consider asking if they learned or did anything interesting that day. You will find this is a great starting point for conversation.

You can also start the conversation by sharing something that you learned or did that day.

- Have a rule of no evil speaking at the table (that means no arguing, insulting or speaking bad about other people. Often this means we don't talk about politics :)

- Have your children help you clean up the dishes and put away the food after dinner.

FAMILY RECITAL/PLAYS AND PERFORMANCES

At one point in our homeschool, we had several children taking music lessons, children were doing projects, and I was being creative. We decided to have a family recital night each week. This provided a time for family to share their creations.

We had plays, puppet shows, project presentations, musical performances and more. This gave dad an opportunity to participate with homeschool. This also gave my children a friendly audience to perform in front of while they build their confidence. A side note, dad got to find out what they were learning.

With our younger children we would encourage them to come up with stories to dress up and make props and put on a play or performance. I have fond memories doing this as a child with my siblings and I also have fond memories watching my children perform.

CULTURAL ARTS

We studied art, music and poetry in Power of an Hour. This was art history and art appreciation, music history and music appreciation, and poetry history and appreciation. Then we checked when the free concerts were at the local universities. We took advantage of cultural fairs and our family loves visits to historic, science and art museums.

We also enjoy listening to a variety of music in our home, as well as having regular family movie nights and reading books together as a family. All of these activities can increase your family's appreciation of the cultural arts.

WILD DAYS

We did not want the children to suffer from nature deficit disorder, so we included Wild Days. These Wild Days were daily neighborhood walks, sometimes canyon walks, and park days on Friday afternoons.

We also enjoy evening wind down walks as a family where we continued the discussions from the dinner table while enjoying some fresh air before bed. When we do this we all sleep batter.

CRAZY DAYS

When I was young I would ask my mom where she was going, she would say, "Crazy, Wanna Come along?" We went on errands, sometimes to the beach, a museum or for a hike, to the grocery store, to a matinee play, musical or concert. So, Crazy Days are about field trips and
getting out in the community.

Also included in this were taking random classes. Once, I took an introduction to Hebrew weekend course with my mother at a favorite liberal arts college. Another time, we decided it would be fun to take a cake decorating course together. These crazy day activities and classes brought us closer together and were a whole lot of fun.

FAMILY TRADITIONS

Family traditions are what bind us together as a family. Some people are raised with lots of great traditions in their home, and others sadly are not. To those who weren't raised with great family traditions, we would like you to know that It is never too early or too late to start some good family traditions of your own. Here are a few traditions we would recommend considering for your family:

FAMILY SCRIPTURE STUDY

We wanted my children to have a measuring rod to determine right from wrong. For us, that was daily scripture study. Each family member got a turn to read. Nonreaders lapread one verse with mom and readers got five verses to read. This helped my children value their faith, learn their faith, have a measuring rod for truth, and confidence reading aloud.

FAMILY PRAYER

We knelt together in family prayer at the end of the day. We expressed our gratitude and asked for needed help. When we were finished, we had a family hug.

These moments communicated our love for God and each other. These moments also taught us to look for God's hand in our life and to be grateful.

FAMILY HOLIDAYS

We made our own family holidays. We celebrate family birthdays, and now that six of seven children are married, we celebrate anniversaries too. We celebrated PI day and one of the children chose it as their wedding day.

We have ancestors that had a shipwreck 16 September 1831 off the coast of Virginia while immigrating to America. So, we celebrate a family Shipwreck Thanksgiving every 16 September and retell the harrowing story.

HOLIDAYS

Our family gathers together to celebrate national holidays and religious holidays. Each holiday has certain traditions associated with them. For example for Christmas we try to make as many of our gifts as we can, so that our gifts are more meaningful. This has resulted in much creativity and family treasures over the years.

We also make lots of homemade candies and goodies together that we share with our friends, family and neighbors. Another special Christmas tradition in our home is that we put a great emphasis on serving at this time with fun service traditions that we do as a family to prepare the way for our Savior.

Again, if you see traditions that others have, that you would love to implement in your home, just do it. It is always a good time to try out a new tradition to see if it will be a good fit for your family.

If you find that you and your children are struggling with your homeschooling, we would advise you to go back and reassess how you are doing with your home culture. We know that we have listed a lot here. And no one is expected to be perfect in all these areas right off the bat. However, as you work together as a family to strengthen the areas that we have listed above, one step at a time, you will see a vast improvement in your homeschool success and overall home life.

7 MOM CARE WHILE HOMESCHOOLING

When you get on an airplane to fly to a destination, before the plane takes off flight attendants always give the same speech. In this speech, they inform you about the rules about wearing seat belts during take off, landing and bumpy times in the flights. They mention there is not smoking and where the bathrooms are. Then they discuss what to do in the case of an emergency. It is here that they explain that in the case that you need oxygen, parents are instructed to put their mask on first, then to help put the masks on their children.

Why is it so important to put your own mask on first? For the simple reason that if you are deprived of air and pass out you will be useless in helping your children.

When we do not take care of our real and valid needs, FIRST, we will soon not be able to help our children with their needs. Moms please understand that self care is not a luxury to get around to only if you find the extra time. It is also not a vanity that only those who are self centered indulge in. Self -care is a necessity and should therefore be scheduled into your busy day.

It is a fact, that if you value something you will make time for it. It is also a reality that if you don't schedule something, then odds are it won't happen. Please, when making your daily, weekly and monthly homeschool schedule make sure to schedule time for your mom's care while planning all the things your children need to learn, grow and thrive.

This mom care time can happen before your children wake up in the morning, during nap/quiet times in the middle of the day, when your children are doing self directed studies, while your children are playing and even after they have gone to bed at night.

A FEW IDEAS FOR YOUR MOM SELF-CARE THAT DON'T TAKE A LOT OF TIME CAN BE:

- Reading good books (even if it's just a few pages at a time)
- Taking your vitamins
- Preparing healthy meals & snacks
- Taking short walks
- Drinking enough water each day
- Enjoying uplifting music
- Daily affirmations
- Keeping a gratitude journal
- Reading scripture
- Messaging/calling a friend (make sure to observe how long you spend on this)
- Doing daily skincare.

It is not how much time you spend that is important. You can fill your inner well and have your needs met in small bursts of time throughout the.

Remember, your self-care times don't have to be extensive to be powerful.

VICTORY LIST INSTEAD OF TO DO LIST

An important part of self-care is reducing the stress in your life. You can do this by creating victory lists and through personal routines.

The purpose of a Victory List is to acknowledge all the good that we do. Oftentimes, moms will compile a To Do List. Then they will eliminate the easy things, but somehow never get to the important things. They could have fifteen things on their list, accomplish fourteen and still feel like a failure as they migrate a task to the next day that never seems to get done.

One day, I took a legal piece of paper and fixed it to the refrigerator door with a magnet. I decided to do the thing that bugged me the most, first. Then throughout the day I wrote down every task I did. I really wanted to see how much I actually do.

It was a detailed list. Instead of writing down laundry, I wrote sorted laundry, washed a white load, dried a white load, folded a white load, and put it away. Then I did the same for a load of colored laundry. I made my bed. I changed diapers. I nursed a baby. I made breakfast, lunch, and dinner. I did scripture study with the children. And I listed everything we did for homeschool.

As the list grew I was amazed. It was almost like the list called to me. You have time to add something else. You have time to relax. You can read. My husband saw the list and said, "You sure got a lot done today!" I smiled and said, "That is like my everyday."

When we focused on victories, a lot more got done.

Even children respond better when we focus on their victories, too. The same with husbands. When we look for victories and take notice, people seem to thrive and grow.

MOM ROUTINES

Several years ago, I spoke at a conference on the west coast. As the keynote, they put me up in a guest cottage in the country. This was so refreshing and stress relieving. When I got home I sat down and did a cluster chart of my life and all the different balls I had in the air, including each family member. My best friend looked at it and said, " I don't see you anywhere on this. Where are you?" I was stunned. She was right. No wonder I was back to stress, I had become invisible to me!

So, my friend and I sat down and talked about what my needs were. Then we put together a new routine. Having family meals was important to me, but even with best intentions, many times dinner was too late or we would be running to grab a rotisserie chicken or something quick. I used to do a menu and I needed to get back in the habit. So, I sat down and wrote a two week menu.

It was summer and here was the schedule I did to take care of things that meant a lot to me:

1. Morning walk - I wanted to be out walking each day. I desired to begin my day with scripture and prayer.

2. Shower, dress, and make my bed

3. Breakfast

4. Start Laundry

5. Dinner Prep - My friend suggested that if I did dinner prep early in the day, or even the night before, it would mean getting dinner on the table on time was more likely to happen.

6. 30 minute timed clean, whatever bugged me the most.
7. 30 minute personal devotional

I was to:

1. Get up before everyone and do my routine when people could not interrupt me.

2. Not tell others what I was doing. Talking about things can steal our steam.

3. No screen time until my list was done.

4. I was to report to her each night, we did the buddy system.

That night, I bought myself an egg timer. The next morning I rose early and headed out the door for my walk. I had written my routine on an index card. When I sat down to do my scripture study, my husband came up to take a shower. He first went to the laundry basket to find some clean underwear. I was embarrassed. That was the first place he looked. But it was empty.

When I had started the laundry that morning, there was already a completed load in the washer I needed to put in the dryer, so I could start a new load. But when I opened the dryer, there was a load in there. So, I took it out of the dryer, and rotated the loads. I folded the under clothes and put them away in the drawers. So, I was sitting with a clear view shot down the hall to our bedroom. I watched him head to the bedroom and open his drawer and he cocked his head with a smile when he found the clothes there. I felt good. You see, I knew that before I could get my children into a routine and my family, ***I needed to set the routines!***

Within about two weeks of doing my routine, it became harder to find what bugged me most that needed being cleaned. My home was looking more orderly. Then I heard my husband rattling around outside. I asked what he was looking for. He said that he figured I was bringing the house to order, he would do the same to his work area and the storage shed. All of this because I focused on the only thing I could change, me!

Since then, I have changed my routine and switched some to the evening. Some parts of the routine my family helps with such as meal prep, laundry, and making dinner. This has been a real blessing to us.

CONNECTING WITH OTHER HOMESCHOOL MOMS LOCALLY AND ONLINE

Lastly, it is important for your self-care as a homeschool mom to create a strong support system. You can do this through connecting with other homeschool moms online and in your community. Having this support can be so helpful when you are having those hard homeschool days and have hit a roadblock in teaching your children.

Having a homeschool support system will help you when you face opposition with friends and family who aren't supportive of your homeschool decision. Having a homeschool support system can give you people to ask for recommendations and reviews of curriculums, books and activities you are considering for your children.

All this is great, just one word of caution. These local and online homeschool groups are filled with mostly women and women can be prone to drama. Don't get caught up in the drama and let yourself be distracted from actually homeschooling your kids.

While we homeschooled and worked to balance "me time" I worked hard to guard our time. Park days gave me an opportunity to meet and socialize with other moms while our children played and we did it "come if you can, no obligation", on Friday afternoons. We also did a once-a-month evening mom homeschool support group. Later, as the children grew, we moms got together for a book group and movie night once a month. All of these are great ways to connect and fill your social needs as a homeschool mom.

8 HOMESCHOOL RESOURCES

Homeschooling today is vastly different than 20 years ago. There is a lot more support thanks to the growing movement of homeschooling across the nation.

There are so many more resources available to parents today. There are lots of great full curriculums, supplemental curriculums for specific subjects, websites, apps, and lots of great books. Here are some of our favorites that we have used with our own families with lots of success and highly recommend.

RECOMMENDED HOMESCHOOL CURRICULUMS

POWER OF AN HOUR

(https://mentoringourown.com/power-of-an-hour-overview/) The Power of an Hour: Gateway to a Classical Education is an all-in-one curriculum. Teach all of your children together in as little as an hour a day.

This includes core subjects of language Arts, Math, Science, History, and Geography; also includes Appreciation and History of Art, Music, and Poetry. Created and Compiled by Donna Goff.

CLASSIC CHARACTER UNIT STUDIES

(https://mentoringourown.com/classic-character-unit-studies-overview/) Classic Character Unit Studies are unit studies based on beloved children's classics. We use the classic to illustrate good character principles.

These Unit Studies include vocabulary words, questions for discussions with your children, activities inspired by the classic, recipes, and more.These were created by Donna Goff, Julia Groves, and Jennifer Wallton. Universal

HOMESCHOOL RECORD KEEPING SYSTEM

(https://mentoringourown.com/catalog/) **This record keeping system created by Donna Goff is not technically a curriculum, however we are including it in this section, as it is a great companion to whatever curriculum you use, to reinforce your children's learning, to keep a proper homeschool record of what your children are learning and to use when creating your children's transcript.** This system includes:

- **The Book of Centuries** is inspired by Charlotte Mason and is a timeline to be built in a binder, spanning 4000 BC to the present and organized by continents. The Book of Centuries becomes like an encyclopedia created by the Aspiring Scholar (elementary aged students).

- **The Book of Nations** is inspired by the Book of Centuries, only for nations of the world and is an encyclopedic gazetteer built by the Aspiring Scholar.

- **The Family Scholar Portfolio** is designed for families and family scholars to track their learning activities and to assist them in setting and tracking learning goals through: victory charts, books read as a family, field trips, activity tracking and more. This helps parents and children in evaluating, setting family goals and rhythms, and tracking progress. The Aspiring Scholar Portfolio builds on the Family Scholar notebook. Family Scholars are those beginning homeschooling and children under the compulsory school attendance age for your state.

- **The Aspiring Scholar Portfolio** is a tracking system for the Aspiring Scholar (mid-elementary age) to track their studies. This is great to use to build transcripts and for those who have to demonstrate what they are studying.

- **The Personal Scholar Portfolio** is a tracking system for the advanced scholar (Junior High, High School, and Adult) to track their studies. This is great for those who are building transcripts and for those who have to demonstrate what they are studying.

LEARNING DYNAMICS.

(https://4weekstoread.com/) Learning Dynamics is the absolute BEST reading program I have come across in the years of homeschooling (and I have tried more than one) This is an easy to use program with lessons you do every other day that will have your kids reading in just 4 weeks.

This program includes a Lesson manual, 53 full-color books, 34 songs, an activity book, Letter rewards, and flashcards. Kids respond to this program to where they beg for the next lesson and gain confidence as they are able to read books starting after lesson 8.

You can find a full review as well a coupon code to save 10% off this program on Julia's family lifestyle blog TheQuietGrove.com (https://thequietgrove.com/teaching-your-kids-to-read-with-learning-dynamics/)

ITALICS BEAUTIFUL HANDWRITING FOR CHILDREN

(https://pennygardner.com/italics/) This curriculum was created by Penny Gardner and I used it with my own children and in my children's art classes.

KHAN ACADEMY

(https://www.KhanAcademy.org/) Khan Academy offers full online curriculums from early learning through High School for core class subjects as well as elective courses like programming and creative writing. We have only used it for their math, but I liked how each lesson has a video walk through, practice tests to see how well your children learned that math concept and then a unit study quiz.

LINKEDIN LEARNING

(https://www.lynda.com/) Formerly known as Lynda offers full training courses for a variety of skills like programming, web design, excel, IOS App building, and graphic design. My husband and I have taken several Lynda courses for learning different Adobe programs (Illustrator, PhotoShop, & Flash) which we use for our Illustrating, graphic design and animations for our work.

This site offers amazing online courses for your kids to learn high demand electron skills.

(some libraries offer free access to Lynda, so double check to see if yours does before signing up for an account.)

GREAT COURSES

https://www.TheGreatCourses.Com/ Great Courses uses the top 1% of college professors to create their high school, college and continuing education courses which are available online.

RECOMMENDED HOMESCHOOL WEBSITES & APPS

HSLDA.COM

(https://hslda.org/) - The Homeschool Legal Defense (HSLDA) website, as we stated earlier in the book, is a great place to go find out what the current up to date homeschool laws and regulations are for your state. For those who sign up for their association they also provide homeschool legal counsel and defense in case you need it as well as current homeschool news that may affect you and your homeschooling effort.

MENTORING OUR OWN

(https://MentoringOurOwn.Com/) Mentoring Our Own is Donna Goff's homeschool lifestyle site created to help moms succeed in homeschool, home, family, and life. She publishes a weekly newsletter connected to this site with great ideas and articles to help moms with their homeschool journey. This site is where you can learn about and purchase the Power of an Hour curriculum, Classic Character Unit Studies, and Universal Homeschool Record Keeping System. She mentors homeschooling moms.

Her Premium Membership includes access to a fifteen hour, three day online Homeschool Power Conference and private online community.

THE QUIET GROVE

(https://TheQuietGrove.Com/) This is the family lifestyle site created by Julia Groves. It is not strictly filled with homeschool content, but does have some great homeschool resources and articles. Including a list of companies that offer teacher and student discounts to homeschoolers and free printable US Geography worksheets.

Otherwise, her site is full of general content to help today's mom. With content on home & family, family travel, DIY, recipes, product reviews, free printables and more.

SHEPPARD SOFTWARE

(http://SheppardSoftware.Com/) The SheppardSoftware is a website that offers a ton of free educational activities for a variety of subjects. However, the main subject I love this site for is for their Geography resources.

In college, I had to memorize the world map (all the nation-states of the world) in just a week. While others attempted to do so by staring endlessly at a world map I was able to do so in less than 3 days utilizing the interactive activities on this website.

ABC MOUSE & ADVENTURE ACADEMY

(https://www.abcmouse.com/abt/homepage & https://www.adventureacademy.com/) ABC Mouse & Adventure Academy are both websites & apps that were created by the same people (ABC mouse is for younger kids and Adventure Academy is for older) These sites and apps have a yearly subscription and offer a bunch of fun activities and games that reinforce a lot of your core subjects in a fun and memorable way.

DUOLINGO

(https://www.Duolingo.Com/) The Duolingo site is a free resource to help you learn foreign languages. We haven't used it personally. However, we have had family and friends use it, and they have had great things to say about it.

HECOA

(https://HECOA.Com/) The Home Education Council of America (HECOA) website hosts FREE online Conferences three times a year: Spring Ultimate Homeschool BootCamp, Fall Annual Not-Back-to-School Summit, and Winter Special Needs Conference.

They have a vast online archive of over a decade of the top homeschool presenters' videos on a large variety of homeschool topics.

MATH ANTICS

(https://MathAntics.Com/) Math Antics: Basic Math Videos and Worksheets offers resources to teach math in a clear way and with humor.

DEGREED

(https://Degreed.Com/) Degreed is a Lifelong learning platform; free to individuals. It is a place to curate your learning path of degrees and courses, online learning, books, articles, and more/. Basically it's a site that helps you create an educational resume that includes more than just formal schooling, but private courses, book read, training and more.

Your profile on this site tracks your learning and can be used to create a resume that truly reflects your skill sets and knowledge base.

PROJECT GUTENBERG

(http://www.gutenberg.org/) Project Gutenberg is a site where you can go and find out digital versions of great out of print books. Some of the books are hard to find right now to buy from the store or borrow from the library.

RECOMMENDED HOMESCHOOL BOOKS

BOOKS ON EDUCATIONAL PHILOSOPHIES

Charlotte Mason Philosophy
- **Charlotte Mason Original Homeschooling Series** by Charlotte Mason –
- **A Charlotte Mason Companion: A Personal Reflection on the Gentle Art of Learning** by Karen Andreola –
- **For the Children's Sake** by Susan Schaeffer Macaully
- **The Charlotte Mason Study Guide** by Penny Gardner
- **A Charlotte Mason educations: A Homeschooling Manual** by Catherine Levison

The Closing of the American Mind by Allan Bloom

Cultural Literacy by E. D. Hirsch, Jr.

Dumbing Us Down by John Taylor Gatto

Home Grown Kids: A Practical Handbook for Teaching Your Children at Home by Raymond Moore

Homeschooling For Excellence by David and Micki Colfax

How Children Learn by John Holt

Leadership Education
- **A Thomas Jefferson Education: Teaching a Generation of Leaders for the Twenty-first Century** by Oliver DeMille
- **Leadership education: The Phases of Learning** by Oliver DeMille and Rachel DeMille
- **A Thomas Jefferson education for Teens** by Oliver DeMille

The Marva Collins Way, by Marva Collins

The One Minute School Teacher by Spencer Johnson
http://www.hoyletutoring.com/Docs/Benezet_The_Teaching_of_Arithmetic.pdf Louis Benezet –

The Teaching of Arithmetic I: The Story of an experiment L.P. Benezet, Superintendent of Schools, Manchester, New Hampshire Originally published in the Journal of the National Education Association, Volume 24, Number 8, November 1935, pp. 241-244 [This is an online article about teaching Math and Language Arts in the elementary years.]

BOOKS TO USE IN YOUR HOMESCHOOL BOOKS TO USE FOR MATH & SCIENCE

175 Science Experiments to Amuse and Amaze Your Friends by Brenda Walpole

All the Math You Will Ever Need to Know: A Self-teaching Guide by Steve Slavin String,

Animalia by Graeme Base

Animals Born Alive and Well by Ruth Heller

The Ben Franklin Book of Easy and Incredible Experiments: A Ben Franklin Institute Science Museum Book

Chickens Aren't the Only Ones: A Book About Animals Who Lay Eggs by Ruth Heller

Math for Your First and Second Grader: How to Be Your Child's Best Teacher by Steve Slavin

Math Yellow Pages for Students and Teachers by Kid's Stuff, Jean Signor (Editor) and Marta Drayton (Illustrator)

Mathematicians are People, too!. Vol 1 and 2 by Leutta Reimer and Wilbert Reimer

The Reason For a Flower: A Book About Flowers, Pollen and Seeds by Ruth Heller

Science Yellow Pages for Students and Teachers by Kid's Stuff, Jean Signor (Editor) and Marta Drayton (Illustrator)

String, Straight-Edge and Shadow: The History of Geometry by Julia Diggins

Wild Days: Creating Discovery Journals by Karen Rackliffe

BOOKS TO USE FOR SOCIAL STUDIES & HISTORY

5 Thousand Year Leap by Cleon Skousen

Childhood Biographies of Famous Americans

Spiritual Lives of Great Composers by Patrick Cavanaugh

The Story of Liberty by Charles Coffin

Sweet Land of Liberty by Charles Coffin Books to use for

Drawing Drawing with Children: A Creative Teaching and Learning Method that Works for Adults Too by Mona Brookes

Drawing for Older Children and Teens: A Creative Method for Adult Beginners, Too By Mona Brookes

Drawing on the Right Side of the Brain: A Course for Enhancing Creativity and Artistic Confidence by Betty Edward

BOOKS TO USE FOR WRITING & LITERATURE

A Cache of Jewels: And Other Collective Nouns by Ruth Heller

Any Child Can Write: An At Home Guide to Enhancing Your Child's Elementary Education by Harvey S. Wiener

The Book of Virtues: A Treasury of Great Moral Stories by William J. Bennett

The Children's Book of Heroes by William J. Bennet

The Children's Book of Virtue by William J. Bennett (Editor) and Michael Hague (Illustrator)

A Child's Treasury of Poems by Mark Daniel

Eagles Wings Comprehensive Handbook of Phonics for Spelling, Reading, and Writing by Susan Mortimer and Betty Smith [Especially, Unit 8 Focusing on Penmanship, Writing, and Book Reports- This chapter alone made this resource valuable]

Eats, Shoots & Leaves: Why, Commas Really Do Make a Difference by Lynne Truss, Illustrated by Bonnie Timmons

Everyday Graces by Karen Santorum

Read Aloud Handbook by Jim Trelease

Tales from Shakespeare by Charles and Mary Lamb

Writing Yellow Pages for Students and Teachers by Kid's Stuff, Jean Signor (Editor) and Marta Drayton (Illustrator)

The Walker Book of Read Aloud Rhymes For the Very Young by Jack Prelutsky and Marc Brown

BOOKS TO USE FOR RESEARCH

The Grocery Store Game by Janine Bolon

Noah Webster's American Dictionary of the English Language, 1828 Facsimile Edition

RECOMMENDED HOMESCHOOL TOOLS

OSMANO JUNIORSCOPE

(https://www.microscope.com/juniorscope-the-ultimate-kids-microscope-1.html) This microscope is a great tool for your homeschool science. It is a quality microscope built to be sturdy for kids 8+ to handle.

With magnification ability of 40, 100 & 400X you can use it for a closer look at everything from money to bugs and leaves to germs. This kit comes with 5 prepared slides and 5 blanks as well as tools and instructions to help your kids prepare those black slides for a variety of subject matter.

BOOGIE BOARDS

(https://myboogieboard.com/) Boogie boards are simple drawing/writing tablets that your children can draw on with a stylus and then click on a button to erase. Our children use boogie boards instead of scrap paper to figure out problems they are working on.

DESKTOPS, LAPTOPS & TABLETS

Whether you prefer Mac or PC computers, IOS or Android Tablets, just make sure the device you are looking to purchase has the ability to access and run all the sites and programs you are planning to use it for. For instance if you are planning to use your device to learn programming, or graphic design you will need a certain quality of processing ability and video cards.

GLOBES/MAPS

You can purchase Globes or Maps in various sizes at both local and online stores. Just make sure the one you get is current (since we all know borders and country names change.)

IN CLOSING

While this book was not a practical application book for how to homeschool your children, we hope we were able to answer your questions on how to get your homeschool set up and started on a good foundation.

Yes, a lot of information was in the pages of this book, but if you take it section by section and set up your homeschool foundation following the advice and principles found in this book you will avoid many of the pitfalls that are common to new homeschool moms, and have a smoother sailing in your homeschool journey.

ABOUT THE AUTHORS

JULIA ANN GROVES

Julia Groves is the third of seven children born to Roger and Donna Goff. She was born in Colorado, but raised predominantly in Utah. Julia was homeschooled from 6th grade through highschool after which she attended George Wythe College. Though she did not formally graduate with a degree, she did maintain a 3.98 GPA during her studies at George Wythe and values what she learned while attending there.

Julia married her best friend Rory Groves in March of 2009 and together they have three young children. In addition to homeschooling their children, Julia and her husband also run their own business. (Rory is an illustrator and Julia runs a family lifestyle site where she enjoys creating resources for today's mom.) In 2015, Julia and Rory sold their home and most of their possessions to travel full time with their children. They spent 6 months living abroad in Europe and then returned back to the US. Though their travels have now slowed down and they are once again looking to settle down in a home that love of travel is still there.

As a born storyteller, Julia has always been fascinated with history, art, different cultures and meeting new people. Additionally, Julia enjoys photography, cooking, experiencing new things, teaching, reading, crafting, travel and graphic design.

DONNA GOFF

Donna Goff and her husband, Roger, are parents of seven children and have homeschooled since the 1980s. They are the grandparents to thirteen grandchildren, twelve living. Donna earned her BA in Fine Art & Design; Drawing & Painting; and earned her MA Ed in 2008 while homeschooling her youngest three children.

She has worked to give homeschool support since 1983 and has been active in presenting at homeschool conferences around the US since 1995.

Donna loves to spend time with her family, to enjoy nature with her family, and spending time with friends. In her spare time, she loves to create art, cook, sew, garden, DIY, sing, write, is an avid walker and enjoys learning new things.